My First Time

Erotic hot stories from a virgin becoming sex addicted. A story of sexy women, explicit taboo, BDSM, erotica swingers and threesomes.

Chapter one

There was one thing that Aryann Tyler despised most.

Party!

Especially when Nicole Carson was the organizer. She stood in front of her house staring at everyone in disbelief. Some young boys and girls were dancing outside, the girls half nude.

She sighed and walked into the living room, it was a total mess, some were dancing and some were making out, her eyes darted to a couch, there she saw a guy taking a girl from behind, he was slamming into her relentlessly and she seem to be enjoying it. Doesn't it hurt?

"Hey prude! A guy called, she recognized him to be one of Nicole's friends because that was their nickname for her.

Aryann hurried up the stairs and rushed into her bedroom, shutting the door.

Taking a deep breath, she sat on her bed, her mom, Susan Carson and her husband Edward Carson weren't spending the night at home, Susan had always reprimanded Nicole against throwing parties but Nicole wouldn't listen.

She brought out one of her novels," Pride and prejudice"

Great idea! This would surely make the night end quickly.

The volume of the music downstairs increased and it was as if the house was going to fall down .She stared at the first page of the novel, nothing was making any sense.

"Damn it! "she exclaimed and stormed out of her bedroom, she walked up to Nicole's bedroom and knocked, she knocked again and again but no one answered, she held the doorknob and realized that the door wasn't locked, she bent it and walked into the room.

"Nicole, the par......."Her words were cut off on seeing her underneath a boy, writhing, sweating and begging. She was shocked at he sight in front of her. She knew Nicole's boyfriend but the guy atop her wasn't Jason .Just how many boyfriends did this bitch has?

"Aryann, what the fuck do you want? Nicole asked, angrily.

"I just think this party need to come to an end, Mom won't be pleased by this and I can't sleep". Aryann replied calmly, she felt pissed that the guy was still digging in and out of Nicole despite the fact that she was standing there.

"I'm not gonna end this party because of you. If you aren't cool with it, go fuck yourself or something! "Nicole screamed and continued moaning.

Aryann slowly left the room. What was she thinking? Nicole had never listened to her, she had never listened to anybody.

Aryann sat on her bed and brought out her cellphone, she stared at the amount on her savings account and smiled. soon, she'd leave this house and would never have to put up with these disgusting parties and erotic scenes.

Luca Anthony Herron slowly came to a halt in front of a restaurant, he got down and gave the valet his car mobiliser.

"Luca". Someone called.

He slowly turned around. It was Ava.

"Are you stalking me now?"

"I just want us to talk".

"I believe we have nothing to talk about".

"We do, let's go in".

"I didn't come here to talk to you but I'll give you the opportunity of talking to me out here".

Ava rubbed her hands. "It's cold".

"I know". He replied sarcastically.

"Well, in moments like this, the man is supposed to take care of the woman by doing things like lending her his coat".

Luca scoffed. "who cares about gender roles when it's this cold".

Ava sighed. "Don't you want me anymore?"

"I thought I made that clear yesterday". Luca reminded.

"It's just that, I still want you, you said I was good in bed and so are you, we don't have to......."

"Let me make one thing clear, I'm not good in bed, I'm perfect in bed and also I told you from the start that once I get tired of you, you'll have to leave so don't try to go against that, if I catch you stalking me again, I'll ruin you! "He threatened, seeing her frightened made him satisfied.

" Have a nice life miss......."He paused and thought for a while. "sorry I've forgotten your name". With that, he walked into the restaurant with a smirk.

Harry Borrison smiled on seeing Luca.

"If it isn't Mr perfect".

Luca frowned and sat down opposite Harry.

"You don't have to tell everyone that I'm perfect, you know".

Harry scoffed and poured a bottle of whiskey into two wine glasses.

Luca picked up his wine glass and stared at it intensely.

Harry grinned. "Do you like the whiskey I chose?"

"No. I like the reflection of my face on the glass "He replied still staring at it.

Harry sighed.

"She thought a man like me would just get tied down with a woman like her". Luca began

"And who's that woman? "Harry asked, curiously.

"Ava, I told her to pack her things and leave yesterday but she was pleading to stay. Well, I can't blame her cause she would never find a man who'd make her scream like I did".

"Luca, don't you ever get tired of this?"

"Of what?"

"Of buying women like clothes?"

"You see, you won't understand, having a woman at my house at all times is very convenient to me, it's not like I'm doing anything wrong, I pay her good money, she enjoys the time she spends with me and when I get tired, she leaves and a new woman comes in. I wouldn't want to be in a scandal like Lewis, a reporter caught him in a brothel".

"That's not what I'm saying, you need a woman who……."

"Okay, I know where this is heading, I've got rules, Harry. I live by my rules, how can I be perfect if I don't live by them?"

Harry shook his head. "Stupid rules".

"What did you just say?"

"Nothing, your rules are great".

Luca nodded in agreement. "so why did you want to meet up?"

"It's about Edward". Harry announced. "He obviously can't pay back the money". He added and swallowed the lump on his throat on seeing Luca's eyes flash dangerously.

"I can't just let him have my money, life is about giving and taking. If he wants this the hard way then I'll do it the hard way!"

Brrrrrrinnnnnnnggg!

An alarm clock clang in a dark room, Aryann slowly brought her hand to it shutting it down then she stood up from bed and turned on the lights. She yawned lazily wondering when she had slept off last night.

"ARYANN!"A voice called from downstairs, it sounded angry.

She quickly rushed out of her bedroom and hurried downstairs to see Susan and Edward staring at the living room in disbelief.

"Morning mother". She greeted uneasily.

Susan huffed. "You can't even do anything right. I told you not to let Nicole throw parties anymore".

Aryann sighed, she always get blamed for Nicole's wrongdoings.

"I tried……"

"Just shut up and tidy up this place". Susan snapped and walked away.

Edward gave her an annoying look and walked off.

Aryann looked around the living room, she always clean up after Nicole's parties. How fair is that? She walked up the stairs to get the waste bin.

Her footsteps came to a halt in front of Nicole's door.

"Nicole, I don't like it when you sleep around, I mean you have a boyfriend for God's sake".

"C'mon Mom, I'm eighteen, I can do whatever I like, and besides I have to try out other guy's aside Jason. I need to know what they all feel like".

Susan chuckled. "I don't want you partying anymore".

"For the love of God, you're not the one always cleaning up, are you?

Susan sighed, she knew she could never win against this daughter of hers.

Aryann walked away, she got the waste bin and started cleaning up the house, life had always been unfair to her…….

The family sat in silence eating breakfast, only the beep sound of Nicole's phone was heard as she kept on chatting with Heaven knows who.

"Mom, I wanna move out next week". Aryann announced.

They all turned to face her in disbelief.

"Why?"

"I'm twenty-one and I want to be independent".

"She's lying, mom, she wants to get away from all of us". Nicole accused.

"Is this how you repay my generosity for taking in someone else's child? "Edward asked, angrily.

"It's just…… I….."

"You're going nowhere, young lady. Who's gonna take care of the house? "Susan asked.

Aryann huffed. "Fine, let me be honest with you all, I'm tired of this maltreatment, the only reason why you want me in this house is to be your house help, you don't even consider me as family."

Susan sighed. Aryann, I do consider you as……..

A crashing sound was heard from the living room, they rushed towards there to see Luca Anthony Herron and some men dressed in black suits, the men were holding guns except Luca. They'd broken the front door.

"Hello Edward, can we talk?" Luca asked, coldly.

Edward shakenly turned to face Susan.

"Take the girls upstairs". He ordered and the women walked away.

Luca sat on a couch, majestically.

"Nice house". He commented

"If….if it's about the money……"

"It's always about the money, old crook, it's been two fucking years and I'm not leaving till you give me my money".

"I…..I don't have all of it but…."

"I want all of it!"

Edward ran a hand through his hair frantically.

"I gave you enough time to pay back, now if you don't have the money, things could get ugly". He warned and gestured to one of his men to start breaking things.

Edward watched in disbelief as one of Luca's men strode towards the TV and smashed it to the ground. He felt helpless, what should he do? He didn't have all of Luca's money and the money he had wasn't even up to half the cash he borrowed.

"I'll do anything you want, Luca, please stop."

Luca smirked." Anything?" He asked mischievously.

"Yes."

He looked around the living room then he saw a picture of Nicole, perfect timing! just when he needed a new plaything.

"Your daughter. "He announced.

Cold terror ran through Edward, he couldn't give Nicole to this beast. Nicole was his priceless jewel, his eyes caught a picture of Aryann.

"You see, Nicole is just eighteen and might be too inexperienced for you, but her elder sister is twenty-one, I think she'll fit right in." Edward explained pointing at Aryann's picture. Luca stared at it, she was more beautiful, and she was worth his money.

" We have a deal then, I'll give you an hour to talk to her."

"So soon?" Edward asked, shocked. Aryann could be stubborn at times.

"Yes and I'll be waiting in my car." With that, he walked off leaving his guards behind.

"I thought you paid him already?" Susan asked as Edward walked into the bedroom.

"How could I when all you and Nicole did was to go shopping every weekend?"

"What are you going to do now?"

"He wants Aryann!" Edward announced.

"What? you know Aryann would never agree to this"

"I don't have a choice, he was going to destroy everything in this God damn house."

"What is he going to do to Aryann?"

"I don't know and I don't care. Don't fucking act as if you care about her, okay? I need her now to repay me for taking her in and you're gonna talk to her, ASAP!"

"What if she doesn't agree to this?"

"She has to. Tell her Luca would kill us all if she doesn't, just tell her anything. Everyone knows Luca well enough, he'll ruin me, if you don't want us to become paupers overnight then you have to convince her to agree to this."

Susan swallowed. she couldn't go back to who she was before.

Aryann sat on her bed nervously, what was that ruthless billionaire doing in her home? She had heard stories about him, there was a time a waitress had mistakenly spilled coffee on his shoe, he had made her lick it off with her tongue. Another time, he'd told a lady to use her shirt to clean his car simply because she touched it.

She had seen him online, he was quite popular in Chicago but then she never thought she would see him face to face in her home. He looked so frosty and his men were holding guns. Fear crept through her veins. Did Edward offend him? Was he here to kill them?

A sound came from the door, she frozed. Then Susan walked in.

Aryann sighed, relieved." Is he gone?"

"No." Susan replied and sat beside her.

"What does he want?" Aryann asked, frantically.

"You!" Susan announced.

Aryann frowned. "He doesn't know me."

Susan slowly turned to face her." Edward was a friend of Luca's father so when his company experienced bankruptcy two years ago, Luca was the only one he could run to, he borrowed a large sum of money from Luca and he hasn't been able to pay back the money, that's why Luca is here, he wants his money but Edward doesn't have it so he wants you instead."

Tears stung Aryann's eyes. "I have nothing to do with this, I'm not….."

Susan quickly held her hands." My dear, I know we haven't been that nice to you but we need you now, you saw the guns, right? If you don't go with him, he's going to kill us all including you."

Shockwaves rolled through Aryann."Wh….What?"

"Yes, he'll kill all of us." Susan repeated.

Aryann swallowed hard." But what would he want to do with me?"

"I don't know but you have to be anything he wants you to be."

"For how long?" Aryann choked out with tears rolling down her cheeks.

Tears dropped from Susan's eyes." I don't know, my child."

"Th…This isn't fair, I didn't do anything wrong, why am I being punished like this?"

Susan pulled her into her arms cradling her hair as she wept uncontrollably, she knew Aryann had a soft heart and would never do anything that would hurt them.

Aryann cried bitterly.

All this while, she had being modest, waiting for her 'Mr right' to show her what true love feels like. Now all her dreams were about to get blown up in her face. She knew that she could never live with the fact that her family died when she could do something to save them and she won't be spared from his wrath too, he'll kill her as well, he'll wipe out an entire family. Even if they weren't nice to her, they were still her family, the people she grew up with and it was up to her to save them.

Luca stared at his new plaything from his car, she was beautiful.

"I'm sorry, Aryann." Edward said not meaning a word of it.

Aryann stared at the three of them, not that she was gonna miss them but that they had succeeded in ruining her life.

"Take care of yourself." Susan muttered.

She nodded faintly.

"We need to get going, miss. Sir Luca's waiting." one of the hefty men said.

Aryann stared at the house which she had lived since she was little, she had planned on leaving this house and move to a nice little apartment of her own but her plan had been disrupted. she turned around ruefully and the men led her to the awaiting car.

Luca stared at her as she got in, she refused to look at him, she kept on staring at the window.

He smirked, she'll forget everything after he was through with her tonight.

Susan stared as the fleet of cars slowly disappeared from the compound.

"If I had known that it'd be this easy to settle my debts, I'd have given Aryann to him sooner." Edward said, greatly relieved.

"But Dad, you have to employ a maid, I can't do the house chores." Nicole complained.

They stared at Susan who seem deep in thoughts.

"Hun, what's wrong?"

"I just…you know. I feel guilty sending her off to a horrible man like Luca."

"C'mon, she'll be fine, once Luca is done with her, he'll let her go and she'll move on with her life."

Susan sighed.

"Look at the bright side of all this, we're free from Luca's wrath and Aryann won't keep on reminding you of Philip, we'll get a maid to replace her." Edward assured.

Susan smiled, relieved. She was starting to worry about who would do the house chores.

"Everything turned out great." She muttered.

Aryann stared at the mansion in front of her. Wouldn't she get lost inside?

"Get down!" A deep baritone voice instructed.

She held the doorknob.

"I'll see you when I get back." He added.

She quickly got down and watched as the fleet of cars rode away.

"Miss." A bodyguard gestured towards her to go inside, she held her luggage but the man took it from her and started walking into the house.

Aryann followed him, she stared at everywhere in admiration, they came by the living room, it was spacious, she had never seen any house this furnished before.

The man led her into a room.

"The housekeeper took the day off, sir Luca said you can take anything you wanna eat from the kitchen" He said and walked away.

Eat? Aryann didn't feel hungry at all, she stared at the bedroom, it couldn't be compared to hers back home.

Home? she thought, no, she certainly wasn't going back there.

She slowly sat on the bed, she was nervous, anxious, fatigued…..She sighed. How she was feeling right now was indescribable. What did Luca want from her? Did he want her as his plaything? She shivered at the thought of that .She had wanted to lose her virginity to someone whom she loved and who loves her in return, probably on her wedding night with the bedroom covered in roses .She couldn't lose it to a beast but how can she possibly say no to him?

Knock! knock!

Luca looked up from his computer," come in" He instructed.

Harry walked into Luca's office, he slowly sat down on the visitor's chair.

"So were you able to settle things with Edward?"

"Yes"

"Woah! so he had the money but he had been playing around with me" Harry exclaimed.

"He couldn't pay back the money"

Harry frowned." But you just said you settled things with him"

"Yeah, I took one of his daughters" Luca announced.

Harry gasped." What?"

"Is anything wrong with that?"

"Everything's wrong with that, for starters, how old is she?"

"Twenty-one" Luca replied, nonchalantly.

"Twenty-one? She's got her whole life ahead of her, she might have dreams that have suddenly been disrupted. She'll hate you for this"

"I can assure you that when I make her come hard tonight, that hatred would disappear and she would beg for more"

Harry shook his head.

"And for your information, everything I do is right and is for myself, my own good, understand?"

Harry nodded." Yes sir"

Aryann stared at the wall clock, it was almost ten o'clock, she had heard the sound of his cars almost an hour ago, he must've chosen to pardon her. She quickly pulled the duvet over her body, she needed to sleep, she needed to be fast asleep. she heard the sound of the door opening. Too late!

"I know you ain't sleeping" He said, hoarsely." And I also know that this is a lot to take in, blah blah,blah, but don't worry, I'll be the one to make all the moves tonight so relax and enjoy this rare experience, women would kill to be in bed with me" He added, proudly. He walked closer to the bed and pulled off the duvet from her body, she tensed and scurried away but she wasn't fast enough, he held her left ankle and pulled her closer to him.

"Don't you dare fight me! if you try to make another move, I'll take you down roughly and you'd be sore for days" He threatened, angrily.

No woman had ever tried to get away from him.

Tears pricked Aryann's eyes, realizing that there was no way out of this.

"Stay still" He instructed and let go of her ankle, he got into the bed and leaned over her resting on his forearm.

Aryann swallowed hard." Please don't……"

"Shhh, if you love yourself, don't dare me!"

She tried to look away but he held her chin and took her lips with his, taking one nibble then another and another until he grew hungry for more but as hard as he tried to weaken her resistance, she wasn't opening up for him, to allow him taste her, he slowly took his lips and stared at her big brown eyes.

"Kiss me" He ordered, breathlessly.

She stared at him for a while.

"Shhh, if you love yourself, don't dare me!" His words reverberated inside her head, she heaved herself up and pressed her lips to his, he responded immediately, she opened her mouth and allowed him dine in. She tasted so sweet, his arms tightened around her as he kissed her deeply loving how beautifully soft her lips were, he kissed her for a long time and she felt her breath being sucked out of her.

When he finally took his lips away, hers were plump and swollen. He hurriedly took off her shirt then tugged off her shorts, he unhooked her bra throwing everything to the floor, he pulled off her panties.

Aryann lay naked underneath him, she wanted to run and cover herself up but she couldn't, no man had ever seen her like this before, she felt goosebumps popped up on her skin as he ran his hands through her body.

Luca felt his cock strain for release in the confines of his pants, he couldn't wait to bury himself inside her body, he quickly took off his shirt, he stood up from her body and tugged off his pants, his eyes never leaving the sight in front of him, he pulled off his briefs and hurriedly slipped on a condom.

Aryann forced herself to look at him, her heart shook rigorously. He was huge. She was gonna die tonight. She quickly looked away but Luca already caught her staring.

"I know what you're thinking. It's just as perfect as my personality" He smirked.

Perfect my foot! she thought, frantically.

When he mounted the mattress again, he slowly parted her legs.

Aryann's breath hitched when she felt the tip of his manhood at the entrance of her body, he was forcefully trying to slide in.

"Fuck! You're so tight!" He exclaimed and with his next move, he penetrated into her.

The piercing pain made her to cry out.

"It hurts" she cried, tears rolling sideways touching the bed.

Luca's chest tightened seeing her tears, he slowly looked downwards, where their bodies were connected and saw blood.

"You… You were a virgin? He asked, shocked, seeing her tears still coming out in thick sheet gave him the answer he needed. Damn! he had never slept with a virgin and he never wanted to, he always liked women who were experienced and knew how to pleasure him. But now, he was inside a virgin but he didn't want to stop. Maybe he should be more gentle.

He slowly rested on his forearm. He gently slid out then thrust in again, this time deeper, he heard her scream in pains. The muscles in his stomach tightened and he began thrusting in and out of her body, ignoring her pleas.

Soon, the pain started to subside and an incredible pleasure took its place, she raised her hips and started moving to the beat of his thrusts.

Placing her hands on his hard chest. She moaned as she felt the hot velvety length of his, thrusting harder and faster, going deeper.

"Luca!" she mewl as she felt her first orgasm. He stared at her intensely as he found his own release .His body tensed and gently fell on top hers. She could feel the heavy thrumming of his heart against her chest. After a while, his chest stopped heaving and he lifted up his body pulling out of her. She winced at the sudden emptiness.

He stood up from the bed and started to wear his clothes. She pressed her thighs together to dull the ache. She looked down the bed on saw bloodstains on the tangled sheets, she felt weak. She shakily stared at him, he was dressed in his shirt and boxers and was holding his pants. Aryann slowly stood up from the bed, it hurt to walk, she headed towards the bathroom beside the bedroom.

"It won't hurt this much next time" she heard him say but didn't turn around to look at him. Luca pulled off the blood stained sheets and arranged a new mattress on her bed, taking the former sheets, he walked away.

Whilst in the bathroom, she sat on the floor as hot tears rolled down her cheeks. There was even a next time.

Luca stared at his reflection on the mirror, he clad in plain black long sleeves, red suits jacket and pants and black Oxford shoes. He smiled satisfied with his look, he walked out of his dressing room, then through the hallway, his footsteps halted in front of her bedroom door. Was she still in pains? He shook his head, it was none of his business.

He walked down the stairs then saw Maria, his housekeeper, standing at the lobby obviously waiting for him, his eyes darted to her hand. She was holding the blood stained sheets. Damn it! He should've disposed it in a more safer place.

"What's this, Luca?" She asked, curiously.

"Nothing that concerns you" He snapped walking into the kitchen to get his coffee.

"Have you gotten a new woman?"

Luca sighed, he knew she wouldn't stop pestering him till he talks.

"Yes"

"Was she a virgin?"

"Yes"

Maria gasped. "I thought you weren't interested in virgins"

"I didn't know she was a virgin, okay?"

"Who's she? Does she want to be with you? Don't tell me you threatened her or something?"

"How I got her doesn't matter, learn to fucking mind your own business!" Luca yelled drinking from his coffee.

Maria sighed." Is she okay?" She asked, concerned.

"I don't know and I don't care. I'm running late for work and I don't wanna talk about this when I get back" With that, he stormed off.

Aryann eyes opened, she has secretly wished that when she wakes up, she would realize that what happened was a dream. She would wake up in her old bedroom with novels by her side. She looked around and sighed. It wasn't a dream, she had just lost her virginity to a man who saw her as his plaything, tears stung her eyes.

The bedroom door opened and Aryann shot up in the bed, clutching the sheet to her body, heart thumping, she wasn't ready to see Luca so soon. But it was a woman coming into the room with a tray holding pancakes and a glass of orange juice. She placed it down beside Aryann who flushed quite embarrassed but the woman smiled.

Aryann took her to be in her early fifties. She blink and watched as she opened the curtains to let the morning light in.

She walked back to her bedside and sat on her bed.

"Eat up" She urged.

Aryann nodded faintly and started eating, she discovered that she was ravenous, she hadn't eaten lunch and dinner the previous day.

Maria stared at her as she ate hungrily, she seem so different from Luca's past women, so beautiful and fragile, she noticed the dark circles under her eyes, she sighed sadly realizing that she must have cried herself to sleep.

Aryann washed down pancakes with the orange juice.

"Thank you" she muttered.

"I'm Maria Hudgens, the housekeeper."

"Aryann Tyler." she replied unable to say the position she was in the house.

"Do you wanna talk about it?" Maria asked with an encouraging smile.

Aryann stared at her for a while, maybe talking about this might ease the pain. Tearfully, she told her everything that she remembered about herself, how her mother had said her biological father had rejected her when she was a baby, Susan had suffered with her little girl alone for two years then she met Edward who accepted her and her child but he had refused to let Aryann bare his last name. Her mother had Nicole for him and she never felt a mother's love after that, they all despised her, they all treated her like trash. She was like the house help.

And finally, she told her what transpired the previous day.

Maria was in tears after hearing the girl's story, she pulled her into her arms stroking her brown hair, murmuring soothing words to her.

Aryann heaved a deep breath and sniffled then she realized she had soaked Maria's shirt with her tears. She quickly moved away.

"I'm sorry." she muttered, her sobs finally subsiding.

"It's okay, I can't believe you did this for your family after all they did to you."

"Mom said he threatened to kill us all."

Maria sighed, what the hell was wrong with Luca? she knew that even if he made those threats, he didn't mean them.

She held Aryann's hands.

"I can't promise you anything right now but I'd try and talk to him, don't get your hopes up that he'll listen to me, he doesn't listen to anyone. I'll just try to see if he might listen to me." Maria said, calmly.

"Thank you." Aryann replied, gratefully.

Maria hugged her again, she wished Luca would listen to her, Aryann didn't deserve this.

Why does it still feels so different? Luca thought, angrily and rested his back on his swivel

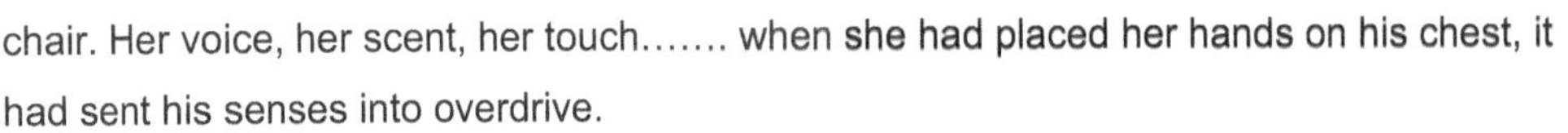

chair. Her voice, her scent, her touch……. when she had placed her hands on his chest, it had sent his senses into overdrive.

And when she had called his name, he wanted her to call his name like that, again and again.

'It's because she was a virgin.' He concluded, that was the best explanation to this. It was different because she was a virgin and now he would make sure she gets all the experience she lacks so that it would be like before, like every other sex he had experienced with his past playthings!

Chapter two

Luca walked into his house, he found Maria sitting on a couch, he started to tiptoe, he wasn't ready for her sermons.

"I know you are home, Luca." She began.

He slowly turned to face her.

Maria stood up." She's just twenty-one."

"So? I'm just eleven years older than her" He reminded, nonchalantly.

"She had nothing to do with the money Edward borrowed" She pressed on.

"I can see that you had some chit chat with her and what do you hope to change? Maria, you have never been interested in any of my women, you always despised them, why are you suddenly interested in her?"

"Cause Aryann's different and she doesn't want to be here"

"There's nothing she can do about this, her father gave her to me, she stays in this house as long as I want her"

"Her stepfather." Maria corrected.

Luca frowned, no wonder Edward had convinced him to take Aryann, he didn't want him to take his real daughter.

He shrugged." She's still like a daughter to him"

Maria sighed." Did you threaten to kill the entire family?"

Luca grimaced slightly." I didn't, I just wanted to wreck the house down, you know. Edward needs to know that he can't mess with me."

Maria figured Susan had said that to make Aryann agree to this.

"Luca, let her go, please" She begged.

Luca walked closer to her.

"I'm warning you for the last time, mind your own business. No one tells me what to do and I'll let her go when I get tired of her, till then, don't you ever tell me to let her go" He warned, sternly.

Maria swallowed and nodded, she stared at him as he walked away. she slowly sat back on the couch, she felt sad that she couldn't do anything for Aryann.

Aryann slowly turned over the next page of 'Jess Promise'. Novels always made her forget about her problems. Someone barged into her room, she looked up to see Luca.

Doesn't he know how to knock?

"I'd appreciate it if you stop whining to my housekeeper" He said, angrily.

Aryann gulped, she silently hoped that Maria wasn't in trouble because of her.

He placed a laptop and some pills on the bed.

"I'm not sick" She snapped.

"And I don't care if you are" He retorted." Those are birth control pills ' cause there might be times when I don't feel like using protection" He explained and smirked on seeing her cheeks grew crimson.

"Let me get some things straightened out here, your father or stepfather or whatever is the reason why you're here not me. So if you're angry, your anger should be directed towards him not me but if you're angry at me that's your problem.

You should be proud that someone like me was your first time, I'm sure I made it perfect for you".

Aryann huffed." Indeed."

Luca shot her an angry look." Are you talking to me?"

She quickly shook her head." No."

"I thought so, let's continue. You're not to leave this house without my permission and secondly, I don't like the clothes on you"

"Am I trapped in here?" She asked, lividly.

"Yes"

"For how long"

"Till I get tired of you"

"When will you get tired of me?" she asked, impatiently.

Luca frowned." That's not up to you to decide. Now back to what we were saying, what's with you and your clothes, are you trying to hide yourself from me or some shit. You should be proud that someone like me wants you in bed"

Aryann stared at her clothes, she was wearing an anorak sweater and plain blue jeans.

"There's nothing wrong with my clothes" She defended.

Luca scoffed and marched towards the closet, opening it,he gasped.

"What are these?" He asked pointing at the clothes.

"Clothes" She replied, calmly.

He pulled out two long skirts and threw them at her.

"Do you know what century we are? who wears long skirts these days? Were you gonna be a nun or something?”

“Probably” She snapped.

“Hey, you should talk to me with respect, okay? I’m not an ordinary man” He warned.

“Yes, Mr Herron” she replied, nonchalantly.

“I didn’t mean you should call me that. Luca is fine by me but when you call my name, call it with respect”

Aryann frowned.” proud peacock” She thought.

“So as I was saying, your dressing issues would be sorted out tomorrow.”

There was no way she was gonna stop dressing this way. she would never dress like a whore to please him. She stared at the laptop.

“Why are you giving me a laptop?” She asked, curiously.

“Well, you need to know how to please me, there are some movies in there, watch and learn, I’ll give you tonight to do all the learning you need, by tomorrow, I want an experienced woman”

Aryann swallowed hard, no one needed to tell her the kind of movies he was talking about. He ran his eyes over what she was wearing again in total disgust then he walked away. Aryann stared at the laptop, angrily.

“I’m not watching anything!” She declared

The morning sun woke Aryann up, she slowly stood up and had a quick bath, then she put on jeans and a faded check shirt.

Her stomach grumbled as she made her way downstairs.

She found Maria in the kitchen setting the table on the breakfast bar.

“Morning ma’m” She greeted, politely.

Maria smiled on seeing her.” You don’t have to call me ma’m, dear. Maria sounds better to me” she replied.

“Alright ma’m, I mean Maria” Aryann corrected and smiled.

Maria loved that smile, she stared at what Aryann was wearing, she really couldn’t be like Luca’s past women, she recalled Ava always walking around the house in just her bra and panties.

“Luca left already” She announced.

“Thank God” Aryann thought and sat on a chair.

“He allows you to call him Luca?”

“Yes and he’s not as mean as you think he is.”

Aryann started eating.” He isn’t just mean, he’s evil, heartless, proud……”

She choked, Maria quickly gave her water.

"Be careful" She warned and sat down on a chair adjacent to Aryann.

"Thank you" she muttered.

"I know Luca is very narcissistic but I do believe that one day, he'll change"

Aryann swallowed the food on her mouth before talking." It's like saying the devil can become a saint"

Maria grinned." He wasn't like this before."

"How long have you known Luca?"

"Since he was five, you see his mother was very promiscuous, she was hardly at home to take care of him so I was like a mother to him. I had wished Luca was my son, you know. He was such a sweet little boy. His father loved his family a lot especially his wife, he always forgave her each time she cheated but she kept on using that against him. When Luca was twelve, his father changed, he became a drunk and he'd always beat up Luca, it was as if he was the cause of his mother's wrongdoings.

On that fateful day, they were going to visit his grandparents, According to Luca, he said he parents were having a heated conversation. His father was distracted and didn't see an incoming truck, they ran into it. His parents died on the spot and he was in coma for almost two months. When he finally woke up, he was devastated. I and Harry, his best friend were the only ones who could go close to him. He was consumed by anger and he shut everyone out of his life."

Aryann sighed deeply. And she thought she had gone through hell in the hands of her family. It was nothing compared to what Luca had been through.

"How did you manage to cope with him?" She asked, curiously.

"Well, it wasn't easy at first since he didn't want anyone around him. I couldn't just leave him alone, he didn't want to stay with any of his relatives, he was young and bad-tempered. Every little thing made him mad and he'd start breaking things. When I got to understand that he wanted everything done his own way, he didn't want anyone to tell him what to do, he wanted people to be scared of him so that no one would dare to step on him .I accepted the new Luca ,it wasn't his fault, I guess he didn't want to turn out like his father."

"He became too evil, I know he went through a lot but he's just so mean" Aryann said.

"I know, dear. I've tried to talk to him but he doesn't listen."

"Has he hurt you before?"

Maria gasped." physically, no. But he had said hurtful words to me, he doesn't mean them"

"He does" Aryann argued.

Maria grinned." Well, I'd like to believe that he doesn't mean them. He turned out a great man, inheriting his father's companies at eighteen. He's so skillful, he has branches all over the globe, I'm proud of him" Maria said, proudly.

Aryann didn't want to voice out her thoughts. Great? He was callous, he oppressed the weak. He might be filthy rich but she'll prefer to be with a barrister who was nice than to be with an evil billionaire.

She couldn't wait for him to get tired of her. She felt warm hands on hers snapping her out of her thoughts.

"Everything would be okay again" Maria said with an encouraging smile.

Aryann nodded, if someone like Maria wasn't in this house, she just couldn't imagine how she'd get through this.

Luca slowly took off his suit jacket, as he undress, he thought about tonight, he couldn't wait to have her again, this time, he will make sure it lasts longer. He didn't expect her to be that good already but she might've learnt some moves. He wore a short and sweatshirt then slipped into a pair of black flip flops. He badly wanted to feel her mouth wrapped around his cock.

He strode towards her bedroom, he held the doorknob but the door was locked. What the hell? Was she actually trying to get away from him?

His fists clenched. she had forgotten who the owner of the house is. He quickly hurried back to his bedroom, he grabbed a bunch of keys. They were spare keys for each rooms in the house. He walked back to her bedroom.

After trying different keys unsuccessfully, a key finally fit in and open the door.

He walked in and saw her lying on the bed with the duvet covering her body Christ! Does she really have to fucking pretend to be asleep every damn time. He hurried towards her and tossed the duvet away from her body.

Aryann tensed, she had heard him trying to open the door some minutes ago, she met his eyes and quickly looked away, he was angry. She slowly sat up.

"Why did you lock the door?" He asked, lividly.

She gulped. "I saw....I saw a rat" Aryann murmured.

"A rat? In my house? Is that the easiest lie you can come up with?"

She suppressed her lips in a tight line not knowing what to say. He held her hand and pulled her up to stand in front of him, he instantly despised the clothes on her body, he had been too busy to take her to the mall today, he wouldn't let it exceed tomorrow because he couldn't stand this clothes.

"I'll overlook what you just did if you prove to me that you're worth it."

Aryann frowned but kept on staring at the floor.

"How?"

Luca's teeth clenched, why was she so clueless?

"Well, for now, let's see what you learnt yesterday" He announced.

Aryann bit her lower lip hard, she didn't learn anything, she didn't even open the laptop.

Luca sat on the bed, he wanted her to make the first move tonight.

"I'm waiting." He said.

She slowly turned around to face him, what should she do first? kiss him? Take off his shirt or short? what if he tells her to suck him? How would she do it?

Luca grimaced seeing the confuse look on her face, he just hope she didn't disobey him.

"You didn't even turn on the laptop, did you?" He asked, hoarsely.

"I didn't" she bit out.

He scoffed and stood up" why?"

"I don't like……"

"It's not about what you like, it's about what I want!" He yelled startling her." The sooner you stop this prudish act of yours, the better for you." He warned.

"Are you tired of me?" She asked, boldly.

Luca smirked.so this was her plan? To make him get tired of her so he would let her go already.

"Let me make this clear, I haven't even started screwing you so you're going nowhere." He declared.

Rage flew through Aryann" You said I'm inexperience, prudish so let me go, you said women would kill to be in bed with you, why don't you get one of those women? I don't wanna go to bed with you. I don't want you! She yelled and quickly close her mouth with her palm realizing who she had raised her voice at.

Luca stared at her in total disbelief. It was time to cut down her wings. He carried her across his shoulder swiftly and headed for the door.

Panic flared." Let me go! what are you gonna do to me?" She yelled struggling but he didn't say anything, his arms tightened around her. As if she weigh nothing, he descended the stairs and headed for the basement.

She kept on screaming and he was sure Maria must have woken up already.

Whilst in the basement, he unceremoniously dumped her on the floor. Her heart was racing. What was he going to do to her?

"No one, I repeat no one dares to talk back at me. You're gonna be in here until you've learnt your lessons and you're ready to do anything I want." With that, he walked out of the basement and shut the door.

Aryann could hear the click sound of the door, he was really locking her in, everywhere was dark, she quickly crawled to the direction of the door and started banging on the door with all her might.

"Please don't leave me in here. It's dark. I won't disobey you again, I won't talk back at you, please open the door." She pleaded, tearfully but heard his footsteps fading. She shakily looked around, it was totally dark and she thought she heard voices.

She screamed and started hitting the door again, if she could get out of here, she would never disobey him again.

"Luca, did you just lock her up in the basement?" Maria asked, angrily.

Luca walked passed her, he wasn't ready to put up with another stubborn woman.

"Give me the keys" Maria demanded.

"Stay out of this, Maria, if you don't wanna get locked up too."

"Just lock me up, Luca. It'd be bearable than knowing that Aryann's locked up in that dark room and I can't do anything about it."

Luca angrily turned to face her.

"You can't do anything about it, Go back to Dreamland and sleep off your worries!" He yelled and walked away.

Tears prickled her eyes.

"I'm so sorry, Aryann." She muttered, helplessly.

Luca could not sleep.

Her voice tormented him, her pleas, her cries.

"Damn it!" He exclaimed and sat up. He couldn't believe she yelled at him, he was going to pardon her for locking the door and disobeying him but she had to fucking yell at him, no one has ever done that, one dared to and she had the nerves to say that she didn't want him.

He had never met a woman who did not want to share something with him but she slammed it at his face that she didn't want him.

He stood up and sat right back, he shouldn't let her out of there, he stared at the wall clock, it was twenty minutes passed midnight, she should be there till 7 o'clock.

"I don't want you!"

The words reverberated inside his head, he stood up and walked in front of his mirror, he stared at himself closely. How could she not want him? He was perfect!

Yes! that was the reason, he was too perfect. She was probably burdened by the fact that he was too perfect.

"Luca, can't you be less perfect." He said pointing at his reflection on the mirror.

He shook his head." I can't, she has to get used to this perfect man and she should be proud" with that, he walked back to the bed and sat down.

"Please don't leave me in here. It's dark, I won't disobey you again. I won't talk back at you, please open the door."

He sighed recalling her pleas. He knew she had already been crying when she pleaded with him. She had been there for almost three hours now. He shouldn't care about anyone but he couldn't get rid of this guilt. He grabbed the keys and hurried out of his bedroom. Immediately, he got to the basement, he inserted the key into the keyhole and gently opened the door to avoid hitting her in case she was behind it.

He opened the door fully and lights from the lobby shone into the basement, he looked around and saw her lying on the cold floor, her body curled. He slowly bent down in front of her and remove some strands of her hair from her face then he saw dried tear marks. She'd cried herself to sleep.

He sighed deeply, why did she still look so beautiful?

He gently carried in his arms, he was extra careful not to wake her up, he walked out of the basement. Maria who hadn't been able to sleep a wink heaved a sigh of relief as she stared from the kitchen at Luca ascending the stairs with Aryann in his arms.

Luca slowly lowered her down into her bed, he covered her with he duvet, she stirred, he quickly stood up to leave but felt her warm hand holding his.

"Did you really had to lock me up in there?" She asked, weakly.

He slowly turned to face her.

"It was so dark, I thought I saw ghosts......."

"There aren't any ghosts in there." He assured.

"I'm scared" She muttered, he saw her lips quiver and he instantly knew that she was gonna cry again.

Without thinking twice, he got into the bed and lay down beside her, then pulled her into his arms. Resting her head on his chest, she wrapped her arms around him. Luca knew she wasn't thinking clearly because she had never been so comfortable around him. Gently, he stroked her hair noticing how soft they were and the lovely scent emanating from her body. Was this him? He didn't even like sleeping in the same bed with a woman after having sex with her but here he was making this woman fall asleep. He knew he couldn't leave her alone tonight.

Aryann woke up with a start, to find strong arms wrapped around her, she realized that her head was resting on a man's chest.
She frozed. Was this Luca?
She looked up and met his cold eyes, he was giving her the" Get up already" look.
She quickly moved away from his body.
"Finally!" He exclaimed and stood up from the bed.
"I thought you were never gonna wake up" He teased.
Aryann stared at the wall clock, it was 9:02am,she slowly recalled what had led to him sleeping in her bed.
Her face flushed." Why didn't you wake me up?"
Luca frowned, why didn't he wake her up? He had woken up more than two hours ago but the thought of waking her up didn't occur to him. Why?
"I can see that you wanna go back to the basement" He threatened and watched as her eyes dilated.
"I….. I'm sorry, I didn't mean to be inquisitive." She quickly apologized but he looked unmoved.
"Are you go lock me up again?" she asked, ruefully.
"Not right now though. If you do everything I want then you'll have no reason to be locked up again" And then, he walked away.
Aryann sighed deeply. she had always had phobia for dark rooms since she was little and what made it worse was her imagination, thinking ghosts or monsters would appear, she couldn't go back to that basement. She just had to be submissive to his demands. All of this would end soon.

Aryann walked into the dinning room, she found Maria setting the table.
"Morning Maria" She greeted, calmly.
Maria walked up to her.

"Are you okay?" she asked, concerned.

Aryann grinned. "I've got a slight headache."

"Oh dear!" She exclaimed and held Aryann's hand.

"Sit" She instructed.

Aryann sat down on a chair.

Maria came back with a bottle of water and aspirin, She opened a flatware in front of Aryann.

"Thank you" she muttered.

Luca walked into the dinning room, he saw her taking two tablets of aspirin. Just how much did she cry at the basement? He was never going to lock her up again.

He slowly pulled a chair backwards and sat down, he stared at her as she ate her omelette, he somehow liked the way her throat flexed as she swallowed.

"After breakfast, get dressed, I need to change those miserable clothes" He began.

"She isn't feeling too well, she needs a good nap today" Maria snapped.

Luca shot her an angry look. Seriously? what the hell was her problem?

"Fine! The clothes would be delivered to you then." He agreed. He didn't have the energy to argue today.

Aryann suppressed her lips in a tight line, she hoped that he wouldn't take it out on her later.

Aryann slowly lay down to sleep, she reached out to a drawer and brought out her cellphone. No calls or texts from her family. She sighed, she was going through hell for them and they just abandoned her. They really didn't care about her. She thought about how Maria stood up for her earlier and smiled. Someone cared about her. Her headache had subsided and it was noon already. How should she spend her day? Her eyes caught the laptop, she quickly looked away from it.

A knock sounded from the door, she stood up, walk towards the door and opened it. She saw two of Luca's guards holding some shopping bags.

"Sir Luca instructed us to bring these to you" one of the guards said.

Aryann moved aside and they walked in, they gently placed the bags on the couch.

"Who picked out the clothes?" She asked, curiously.

"Sir Luca" the other guard replied.

Luca went shopping for her himself? He was really bent on changing her clothes for good.

"He said you should dispose the clothes you came with" with that, they walked away. Aryann scoffed, she couldn't just dispose her clothes like that.

She walked up to the couch and started bringing out the clothes from the shopping bags, they were beautiful, unable to resist the urge to check them out, she started trying them on, she wondered how he knew her exact size, opening more bags, she found high heels, sneakers ,purses and handbags. She slowly sat on the couch, it's not as if she was going to leave this house, he'll never allow her to go out so why did he buy so many clothes and shoes? She stared at the simple flared skirts and dresses, she'd have to stick with those, her eyes darted to the tight and short gowns, what did Luca wanted to turn her into?
She slowly arranged everything inside her closet leaving her old clothes neatly arranged in it too, she just had to make sure Luca doesn't open the closet.
She looked around the bedroom and saw the pills, she had to start taking them immediately, she couldn't get pregnant for someone like Luca, she'll wither and die and Luca too wouldn't want that.
She stared at the laptop, he might come for her tonight and if she doesn't please him well enough, he might lock her up in the basement again.
She quickly sat on her bed and turned on the laptop. Her heart raced at the sight in front of her, from time to time, she'd close her eyes then look again. At some point, she started comparing Luca's crotch to the ones she had seen in the movies. Realizing what she was doing, she turned off the laptop and choked out;
"This is bad!"

Luca walked into the living room, he found Maria watching TV, she stared at him and looked away.
"Now you're giving me the silent treatment" He began.
"I have nothing to say to you" she snapped.
"Why do you care so much about her?"
"Cause she's not like your past women who are rude and proud."
Luca frowned." She has bewitched you" He teased.
Maria scoffed." She did nothing to me and you should start treating her nicely."
"Nice? I'm not nice" He reminded.
"I know I can never convince you to stop sleeping with her but please stop making her feel like a slave, do you like the fact that she's so scared of you?"
Luca nodded." Yes"

She suppressed her lips a tight line." You're impossible."

"Are you're very stubborn, just how many times will I warn you to stop talking about her, do you want me to lock her up in her bedroom at all times so that the two of you would stop this mother and daughter relationship? He asked, angrily.

Maria tensed." please don't, Luca. It hasn't gotten to that" she pleaded.

He smirked." So watch it, old lady" And then, he walked away.

Maria sighed, she had been wishing earnestly for a miracle to change Luca but he keeps on getting worse.

Luca stood in front of Aryann's door, he hoped she had learnt her lessons and would not get him angry tonight. He didn't want to lock her up in the basement again but his mind becomes vague once anger sets in.

He bent the doorknob and walked into the bedroom, she wasn't pretending to be asleep as usual but was sitting on the bed obviously waiting for him.

He stopped dead in his track taking in what she was wearing. she slowly stood up to face him.

His jaw dropped seeing her in just a bra and panties. He tried to pull himself together, he had seen this before, he had seen everything about her.

"Hey ba…..baby" she muttered trying to sound seductive but she fails woefully.

'Baby? 'Luca thought, astonished.

She walked up to him and pushed him to the bed.

'Is she okay? 'He thought again and slowly sat up.

"Take me…..and……em…… grind me now."

Luca chuckled. Grind her? She was clearly forcing herself to say those things. She looked funny doing so.

"I never knew you know how to laugh" Aryann said, amused.

Luca quickly pulled himself together." I wasn't laughing." He snapped." And what the hell is wrong with you? Have you gone nuts? He asked, sternly.

Aryann frozed. He was angry, she did try her best though.

"You said I should watch……"She drawled and pointed at the laptop.

Luca suppressed his lips in a tight line trying hard not to laugh." You watched it? or you glanced through it?

Aryann bit her bottom lip hard, which of the questions should she give a positive answer to?

"Let me guess how you watched them, your eyes were closed from most of the scenes."
She swallowed, he was getting really pissed.
"No wonder you were acting like a clown" He teased.
"I'm…. I'm sorry. I don't know how to seduce you."
She couldn't seduce him but she made him laugh. He shook his head, that shouldn't matter to him. He sat back like an ancient King surveying his concubine.
Heat flared in her belly, she felt his eyes boring into her skin. He held her hand and made her sit on his laps, fitting her thighs on each side of him.
Aryann's heart raced at the intensity of his gaze.
He smirked." I'm gonna grind you like you asked, baby" With that he captured her lips in a devastatingly hot kiss.

His lips left hers." Are you on the pills?" He asked.
Aryann nodded, she had started taking them earlier that day.
He wrapped his arms around her and kissed her again. Her resistant dissolved. Their breath mixed, his taste consumed her mind, their tongue skimming each other's. She moaned into the kiss and he drew her bottom lip into his hot mouth.
His hands explored upwards running through her cleavage. She felt his erection beneath her and rocked against it. He moaned loudly.
His hands gripped her backside, he squeezed hard. He kissed the side of her neck. Realizing how sensitive she was there, she bit her bottom lip hard trying not to moan but when he sucked on her neck, a low moan vibrated in her throat.
He slowly turned her around making her lay flat on the bed. Then he came atop her resting on his arms. He kissed her deeply, the tornado between her legs was strong and sweet and it made her wild.
His tongue found hers and she groaned into his mouth, inhaling his scent while his powerful body held hers. The heat, the dampness, the taste, everything was hard and fast as his lips worked on hers.
He slid his hand into her panties.
"Uhh!" She moaned into his mouth as she felt one of his long fingers inside her body.
Luca smirked ,she had said before that she didn't want him but here she was, so fucking wet for him.
Aryann closed her eyes trying to clear her thoughts, this wasn't her, she shouldn't be enjoying his touch, she shouldn't want this, she couldn't help but love the sweet sensation flowing through her body as his long fingers started plunging in and out of her body.

The innocent way she bit her bottom lip almost drove him insane. He started moving his fingers faster, plunging and circling, eliciting moans of pleasure from her.

He slowly took his fingers away and tugged her panties down her legs, she heaved herself up so he could take off her bra.

Luca stared at her body, he felt he had won a prize beyond price. He could see her ruby hard nipples aching for his touch, for his mouth. He ran a hand through one engorged tip and her breath hitched. He lowered his head and took a nipple into his mouth.

"Luca" She moaned pressing her head back in the pillow. The reality of his mouth on her breast was something she had never known or imagined but felt so incredible.

He knead her other breast in his palm, while she ran her fingers through his hair enjoying the sweet sensation racing through her body.

She was vaguely aware that he was no longer on the bed but was quickly undressing himself. When he climbed into the bed again, he lay beside her.

"Put your hands on me, Aryann, touch me" He instructed.

Aryann felt her heart take a more urgent beat, this was the first time he was calling her by her name. She quickly shook her head. She shouldn't be thinking about that. She rolled to her side and ran her hand through her hard chest wondering where the courage came from, she could feel his heart beat against her palm, she ran her hand downwards caressing his abs.

Luca's breath grew labored feeling her warm little hand running through his body.

Suddenly, she stopped. He stared at her.

"What?"

She suppressed her lips in a tight line and looked away, he grinned seeing her cheeks grew crimson, he understood what the problem was. Slowly, he held her hand and brought it closer to his erection encouraging her to explore him.

Her fingers closed around him and he sucked in a sharp breath.

"We'll have plenty of time to explore, I can't wait any longer" He muttered, breathlessly, She quickly took her hand away from him.

He came atop her again pushing her legs apart. Then slowly, he started sliding into her. Instinctively, she lifted up her hips, he thrust his full length into her.

"Ahhh!" She screamed in ecstasy.

Chapter three

Luca held himself still savoring the feeling of being inside of her ,he felt overwhelmed. Their moans filled the bedroom, he started moving in and out of her, assaulting her womanhood with slow sweet strokes. When he couldn't stand his slow movement, he pounded into her at fast pace, the sound of their skin hitting filled his ears.

She wrapped her arms around his back as his thrust intensified, he grabbed one of her legs and hooked it around his waist so he could move deeper.

Pleasure consumed her at each hot slide of his cock, he was going so deep. She tensed around him. He buried his head in the crook of her neck, his breath staggered, hot and wild against her skin.

She cried out his name as she felt ripples of her orgasm clenching and unclenching around him. He felt his climax ripping through him. He emptied himself inside her, his body shook and clung to hers like an anchor.

With eyes closed, his cheek against her chest. He felt her heart beat against his ear. He focused on it letting it bring him down from the most intense experience of his life.

He opened his eyes and rolled off her body. What just happened? Was that just sex? Why was he feeling so giddy? He should go back to his bedroom now, he should leave but his body was betraying him, he pulled her close to him and covered them both with the duvet.

Aryann tried to sleep, to stop thinking about what just happened, it wasn't like the first time, it had been so intensed that she found herself already fantasizing about the next time. God! what was wrong with her?

He was losing his mind!

He stared at his monitor stunned beyond words at what he had been typing, he had never made any mistake like this before, how was supposed to do the right thing when he was typing and thinking about last night.

In a short period of time, he had broken two of his rules already. He had slept in the same bed with her twice and now he was getting distracted. This was going to stop, this had to stop. Luca Anthony Herron did not act like this. The last thing he needed was some clingy woman ruining everything. She had to stop creeping into his head.

A loud sound sent him falling off his swivel chair, he looked up angrily, it was Harry.

"Where the hell did your mind travel off to? space? I've been calling you for ages, I had to hit something to revive you!" Harry exclaimed sitting down.

"You almost gave me a heart attack." Luca snapped standing up from the floor, he sat on his swivel chair again.

"What were you thinking about?" Harry asked, curiously.

Luca gulped." I…. I was thinking about the party tomorrow."

Harry frowned." Why?"

"I was wondering if everything was arranged already"

"You're not usually concerned about organizing the company's party. I and the marketing team always do that, isn't it strange that you're suddenly….."

It's not strange, do I have to explain myself to you?" Luca asked, harshly.

"No sir" Harry shrugged.

"Why are you here?"

"There's a rumour spreading around the company about you, it might ruin your image if the press gets to know"

"What's going on?"

"Well, since no no has seen you with a woman publicly, I think it was concluded by some gossips that you're either gay or impotent"

Luca frowned." What?"

Harry chuckled." I was amused when I heard it, I mean if they know about your flings, they would call you" Lord of romps" Harry replied still laughing, on seeing Luca's angry eyes, he closed his mouth.

"I'm just saying" He shrugged.

"People can't seem to mind their business, can they?"

"Well, I was thinking that you should show up with a lady tomorrow just to burst their bubbles" Harry suggested.

"I won't, do you want Aryann to get the wrong idea about who she is to me?"

"Aryann? Woah! Her name's pretty" Harry muttered.

His heart clenched, why was Harry admiring her?

"Is she pretty?" Harry asked.

Luca frowned." Why are you asking?"

"I'm just asking so I'd know what to expect tomorrow."

"Who says I'm coming to the party with her?"

"I know you will. Come to think of it, you always tell me about your past flings, so tell me about Aryann" Harry requested.

Luca didn't like the idea of talking about her to Harry at all.

"It's none of your business."

Harry gasped." Have you finally been whipped?"

"I'm not whipped, you moron. Is there anything wrong if I don't wanna talk about her?"

"You've never refused to talk about your past flings, you're always eager to tell me about how they are in bed, if they smell bad and……"

"Harry, leave my office, I have to go back to work!"

Harry grimaced slightly, there was something off with Luca and he'd get to the bottom of it. He smiled cheerfully and stood up." You know the press are always waiting for interesting news about you." He said and walked towards the door then turned around." See you at the party with Aryann" with that, he hurried away.

Luca's fist clenched. He knew this was the only way to stop the rumours from spreading but he somehow had a bad feeling about it.

Aryann stared at the hickey on her neck, she had felt disappointed when she had woken up alone that morning. She knew she shouldn't be but she was expecting his arms wrapped around her once she wakes up.

She stared at her reflection on the mirror, she was turning into someone else, Luca was turning her into someone else, he was pushing her away from herself and everything she knew and truly wanted. She touched the hickey as memories from the night flowed through her mind making her wish it was repeating itself right now.

She slowly sat on the bed.

"What are you doing to me, Luca?"

Luca lay down to sleep, he wouldn't touch her tonight, he would organize his thoughts and reconstruct his brain then last night would mean nothing to him.

He closed his eyes. What was she doing right now? Was she thinking about last night or was she super excited that he won't be coming for her tonight. He angrily sat up, he should go to her, he lay back and covered himself with his duvet but the temptress just doors away was still creeping into his mind.

"This isn't good!"

Aryann stared at Luca walking into the dinning room, his face expressionless, he was clad in blue long sleeves and pair of plain grey pants with black Oxford shoes, the first and second bottons of his sleeves were off making him look dangerously handsome.

He met her gaze and she quickly looked away. Maria walked in and sat on a chair adjacent to her.

"How was your night, dear?" She asked, cheerfully.

Luca held his fork awaiting her reply.

"It was great, I got to finish that book you bought for me, thanks again" She replied lifting a fork full of pancakes to her mouth.

Great? Luca thought, she was indeed happy that he didn't come to take her while he felt tortured.

He glanced at her and saw some syrup on the side of her lips, he suddenly wanted to kiss them off and lay her down on the table pouring the syrup all over her body, then.........

"Luca" Maria called snapping him out of his perverted thought.

"What?" He grunt.

"You said you had something to tell me" she reminded.

"Oh! Help Aryann pick a dress from her closet, I don't want her making a mockery of me 'cause she has no sense of fashion" The moment he said those words, he wished he could take them back seeing her face flushed in embarrassment.

"Why do I need to pick a dress for her?" Maria asked obviously annoyed.

"She's coming to the company's party with me"

"What?" Maria and Aryann asked at the same time.

"Yes, who's got a problem with that?" He asked, harshly.

Aryann gulped, she had always hated parties, she knew it'd not be like the parties Nicole hosted but there would be so many elite members of the society and she might end up making a mockery of him like he said. But there was nothing she could do about it, disobeying him would lead to getting locked up in the basement again.

"One of my drivers would pick you up at seven, see you there" With that, he stood up and walked away.

Maria sighed, she really didn't understand why Luca would want to take Aryann to a party. He usually hated public appearance with any of his playthings.

"Wow! You look so beautiful, my dear" Maria exclaimed walking into Aryann's bedroom. The make up artist was tidying up her things, she was sent by Luca.

"Thank you" Maria said to the make up artist who smiled and walked away. She turned to face Aryann.

"I can't breathe and I don't like......."she trailed off staring at the upper swells of her breasts which were exposed.

Maria chuckled." I know you're quite uncomfortable with the dress but I don't want Luca to get mad at you tonight"

"I'm so nervous, Maria, what if something goes wrong. He might get furious and…….."

Maria quickly held her hands, she wished Aryann wasn't this scared of Luca.

"Nothing would go wrong, just be optimistic, okay?"

Aryann nodded and hugged Maria trying to assure herself that nothing would go wrong.

Luca looked around the hall, just as he wanted the party, he loved the trapping of wealth around him, the expensive scent of the women as they walked passed him with unconcealed looks of interest in his direction.

He smirked. Harry walked up to him.

"Is Aryann still coming?" Harry asked.

His smirk turned into a frown." Will you stop……"His voice trailed off when he saw her looking around obviously looking for him, he caught some men staring at her and his jaw clenched.

Harry followed his gaze and caught him staring at a woman.

Luca's heart raced and his head exploded with pride when she saw him. She started walking up to him.

Her brown hair was done in a French twist, she wore a set of dangling earrings and gold necklace, She was wearing a sleeveless black dress reaching her mid-thigh, he could see the upper swollen of her breasts, this should be what only him could see, why wasn't she wearing a jacket?

His eyes dropped to her feet encased in golden high heel shoes, his desire escalated. He knew he should be okay with the way she was dressed. He was the one who didn't want her wearing her old clothes so why was he pissed that her cleavage were exposed?

As she came closer, he stared at her face, her makeup was moderate and he managed to choke out." You look stunning"

Aryann suppressed her lips in a tight line trying hard not to smile, he looked gorgeous in his black tuxedo.

"I'm Harry" He introduced stretching his hand to her.

"Aryann" She replied and took his hand.

A hard knot twisted in his gut as Luca stared at their skin contact.

"I'm Luca's friend, it's so nice to meet you" Harry said sweetly still holding her hand.

Aryann smiled. She didn't quite believed it when Maria had said Luca had a best friend called Harry, she wondered how he could stand to be around someone like Luca when he seems to be the exact opposite.

Luca stared at Aryann. She smiled. She smiled at Harry. She had never smiled at him before.

'All you do is make her cry' His subconscious mind mocked.

A heavy feeling like a rock made his chest so tight, She looked so beautiful when she smiled, more beautiful, but he wasn't the reason for that.

Anger laced through him." Harry, don't you have somewhere to be?" Luca asked, flatly.

Harry took his hand away from Aryann's. "I don't……"

"You do" Luca interrupted.

Harry frowned." Was this jealousy he sensed in Luca?

He nodded and turned to face Aryann." See you around, Aryann" With that, he walked away.

Luca coldly gestured towards her to sit down, she quickly sat down placing her purse on the table, she didn't do anything wrong, did she? He sat beside her but didn't say anything.

"Mr Herron" Someone called, they looked up to see two men and a lady, they seem to be middle-aged and rich.

Luca stood up, they were some of his board members.

"A pleasant evening to you all, I hope you're enjoying the party."

"Very much, Mr Herron" The lady replied.

Luca could see the men staring lustfully at Aryann. Why can't they keep their eyes to themselves?

He took her Aryann's hand and she stood up.

"She's my girlfriend" He introduced, proudly.

Aryann's eyes bulged, she wasn't quite expecting that.

"She's beautiful" One of the men confessed staring at her cleavage.

Luca's teeth clenched." I know."

They nodded curtly and walked away.

Luca let go of her hand and sat down, she sat down too wondering why he was having mood swings. He just introduced her as his girlfriend, she knew she shouldn't be happy about it but she couldn't help it.

"I didn't mean what I said earlier, I just wanted them to think that way, it doesn't sound right to introduce you as my plaything, does it? so forget I said anything like that" He said, smoothly.

Aryann felt a strong ache inside her chest. She knew that was what she was to him but hearing him say that to her face hurt a lot. She nodded curtly wishing the party would come to an end.

Soon, Luca left to talk to some business partners, she was alone at the table. She stared at the empty glass in front of her, she was thirsty, she looked around, a waiter wasn't close by. She slowly stood up and walked towards the bar stand.

Someone bumped into her and quickly steadied her so she wouldn't fall.

"Aryann? He asked in disbelief.

She looked up at him." Cole" She muttered.

He slowly let go of her taking in what she was wearing.

"I never knew we'd meet again" He began.

Aryann smiled, faintly. Why did they have to meet again at this time of her life?

"Me either" She replied.

"You look so beautiful, I mean you've always been beautiful but tonight it ….. it's just….."He stuttered unable to find the right word to say.

"Thanks" She replied as heat warmed her cheeks.

Cole smiled, he had always enjoyed making her blush, he silently prayed that she wasn't with someone.

Harry walked up to Luca.

"See, everyone is talking about the boss' beautiful girlfriend, my plan worked" He said, triumphantly.

Luca scoffed, he was starting to regret bringing her to this party, she was getting too many attention from men.

Harry looked behind Luca and saw Aryann a bit far from them talking to a guy.

He smirked. It was time to prove if Luca was really getting jealous.

"Oh my God! That guy seem to be really into Aryann, his eyes are all over her body" He announced. Abruptly, Luca turned around.

Hurt ripped through him seeing her laughing with the guy. Does she fucking have to smile and laugh in front of every man except him?

Harry stared at Luca amused, he watched as Luca hurried towards them taking off his jacket.

"You're in trouble, Luca" He muttered.

Luca placed his jacket around her, she stared at him startled by his presence.

"I was looking for you" He began lowering his deep baritone voice.

Cole stared at Luca then at Aryann.

"Are you together?" He asked half hoping and half doubting.

"Yes" Luca replied, proudly. He could see disappointment written all over Cole's face.

"You must know who I am but I don't seem to know you" Luca said.

"Oh! I'm Cole Meyers from KM finance, my boss had an emergency so he sent me instead" Cole replied.

Luca nodded, nonchalantly.

"I should get going now, it was nice seeing you again, Aryann" He said somewhat sadly.

Again? Luca thought.

Aryann smiled." Bye Cole" she muttered equally sad then Cole walked away.

Luca stared at her, why was she sad over that Jackass?

"Dance with me" He offered.

"I'm sorry, I don't know how to dance" She declined," I wanna use the restroom" And then, She hurried off.

Luca stood there for a while feeling like a hundred years old.

Aryann walked into the restroom, to her relief, it was empty, she bent and splashed water on her face. Cole was her first and only boyfriend so far, they hadn't dated for long though, just two months, he was in his final year in high school then and she still had two more years to go. He had told her before that he liked her since junior high but was scared of getting rejected because she had been too modest.

She came to like his generous and cheerful nature and when they started dating, he'd always give her flower, he'd always kiss her on her cheek and few times on the lips and at night, they would be on the phone for hours, he'd sing for her before hanging up.

After his graduation, he left to study in Washington. He had told her he didn't want to go to college there but that was what his parents wanted. He had said if fate wanted them to be together, they would meet again.

Aryann sighed deeply. Fate was seriously playing with her. She was now with a beast till Heaven knows when he'd finally let her go.

A sound came from the door, she glanced at the door to see a woman walking in, she locked the door so that no one else could come in, Aryann didn't feel fear, she felt bemused.

She stood up straight and shook her hands out then wiped her face with a towel.

"Hello dear"

She turned to face the woman and met her dark slumberous eyes, she looked so stunningly beautiful.

"Hey" Aryann replied and turned to walk away.

"I must admit, I was quite surprised to see Luca with a lady publicly" She began.

Aryann's footsteps halted, she slowly turned to face her.

"Sorry, I don't think I know you"

"I'm Ava Dalton and I don't wanna know you, I just wanna warn you, I know you're Luca's new plaything, the one who replaced me, he might be so good that you'll crave for more but it should be nothing more than that, if you get too attached to him, you're only going to end up broken hearted cause once he gets tired of you, he won't hesitate to throw you out of his house"

Aryann's fist clenched." Why are you telling me this?"

"I'll be honest with you, darling. I feel so hurt that he replaced me so soon, I feel hurt that he didn't feel even a thing for me and at the same time, I feel pathetic cause he told me about his rules from the start but I still couldn't help it"

Ava stared at her for a while, she seem confused.

"Oh! you don't know about his rules, his first rule is that no woman should step into his bedroom, second, after sleeping with a woman, he doesn't share the same bed with her till morning. Third, He can never love anyone but himself and lastly, when he lets you go, don't ever think of coming back.

Aryann stood there confused as hell, why then did he sleep in the same bed with her twice? She shouldn't be listening to a depressed woman, even if she knew Ava was saying the truths he didn't want to listen to her bitter truth.

She hurried towards the door and opened it.

To her surprise, Luca was leaning on the wall across the restroom obviously waiting for her, he stood up straight and walked up to her.

He took her arm." What took you so long? Is something wrong? You look pale."

Just then, the door opened again and Ava sauntered out. Aryann took in Luca's reaction with sick fascination. His eyes narrowed and his face flushed.

Luca stared at both women, it was like see a shiny piece of diamond next to dirt. At that moment, he was sure of one thing, Aryann was different.

"Go back to the table!" He ordered.

Without staring at him, she walked away.

"What did you say to her?" He asked, curiously.

"Nothing much, I only told her your rules and that she should never ever think that you'll see her as anything more than a sex-toy" Ava replied boldly.

Rage ran through his body, if only she wasn't a lady, he would have broken her nose. This was insane, she was right but strangely, he didn't want Aryann to think that way.

"For the last time, stop stalking me, I'll overlook this but if you ever approach her again, you'll regret the day you were born, get this into your head, she's not like you" And then, he strode away.

Ava scoffed. No one could be like her, she was irreplaceable!

The ride home was a silent one, Luca glanced at her, she had been staring out through the window. H'd had a bad feeling about bringing her to the party, now it turned out terrible.

"Who was that guy at the party?" He asked, curiously.

Aryann frowned." Cole Meyers" She reminded, flatly.

"He told me his name already. I mean who is he to you?" He pressed on trying to ignore her rude reply.

"He was my boyfriend in high school" She replied still staring at the window. Why was he asking anyway?

Luca recalled the way she had been laughing with him.

"Do you still like him?" He asked, he knew it wasn't his business but couldn't help it.

The car slowly came to a halt in front of the mansion, the driver walked out.

Aryann pulled off his jacket and stretched it to him, she wondered why he had made her wear it in the first place. She wasn't cold. Luca grabbed his jacket from her.

"I asked you a question" He reminded trying to sound neutral.

Aryann angrily turned to face him." Does it matter? Even if I still like him, will it change anything? What's it to you anyway?

Luca teeth clenched." I was just asking cause you should forget about him, as long as I want you, I wouldn't want you thinking about any other man"

Ava's words ran through her head and before she could even think, she spoke." You're messing up my life. You're ruining me and I hate you for that. Just get tired of me already!" She yelled.

Her body trembled on seeing him glaring at her, she just yelled at him again, she couldn't get locked up in the basement, He reached for her but she quickly opened the door and ran into the house.

"ARYANN!" She heard him call but she didn't turn to look at him, she ran as fast as she could cursing the heels she was wearing. As soon as she got into the bedroom, he was already close to the door.

She dashed into the bathroom and locked the door.

"Open this door, Aryann, don't make me break it down!" He yelled.

Shakily, she kicked off her shoes.

"I'm....I'm sorry, I didn't mean to yell at you, I'm so sorry" She begged, tearfully. He was angrier than he looked when he locked her up in the basement that night, she just didn't want to imagine what he might do to her now. She close her mouth with her palm as hot tears rolled down her cheeks. She had promised herself not to make him angry again, she had been doing everything he wanted without complaining but meeting Cole tonight had reminded her that she could never come to terms with this kind of life and then Ava had reminded her that at the end, she was going to feel used.

"If you don't open this door at the count of three, I'm gonna break it down and you'll be sorry" He threatened.

"One"

There was no way out of this. She wouldn't die anyway, she'll only be scared as hell in the basement and if he breaks down the door, he might just add to her punishment.

"Two"

She opened the door and stood in front of him, staring at the floor and expecting him to flung her across his shoulders.

Luca stared at her wet cheek, she had been crying just as he thought. Did she always have to cry everytime? He was sick of it, he was angry at himself for always being the reason for her tears.

He knew some people thought he was a monster but he had never felt like one until tonight when she ran away from him, she had seem so frightened when he reached out to touch her. Was this what Maria had said about her being so scared of him? He now understood what she meant. He wished she could smile at him like she did to Harry and laugh like she did with that Jackass.

He closed the distance between them, his anger fading, then he pulled her into his arms.

Aryann's eyes widened as his scent filled her nostrils, she wasn't expecting this. Wasn't she getting locked up? She thought he was furious a while ago. But here she was in his warmth embrace. She wasn't sure if this was the Luca she knew.

"I'm not a monster so don't run away from me again" He whispered running his hand through her hair.

Aryann got a hint of sadness from his voice.

"Forget whatever Ava told you, listen to only me, you're different from her".

Her heart leapt." Different? How? Don't let his words get to you" Her subconscious mind warned.

He slowly disengaged from her then stared at her cleavage.

"Do you know how many men I caught staring at this?" He gestured to her boobs.

Aryann sent a self-conscious glance at her bust.

"I thought you like these kind of dresses" She reminded, calmly.

"Well I did but I…. never mind" He snapped, he wasn't ready to give her any reason to think that he was jealous. He wasn't jealous, he just didn't want any other man lusting after her. There was a difference between being jealous and being protective, right? Cole's face popped into his mind. Damn it! He had to make her forget about him.

He held her chin, lifting it up, he covered her lips with his. He pulled back and tilted her head to a more accepting angle then kissed her again.

His touch worked on her like a drug, every nerve inside her body was screaming for him, it would be the most obvious lie on earth if she said she didn't crave for his touch, their eyelids fluttered close.

Luca's tongue went deep to dwell with hers and he groaned to how sweet she tasted, his mouth move over hers hungrily, becoming a ruthless pressure dominating her sensual ease.

Aryann kissed him back, her arms were around his neck but she didn't know how and when she had done that. When they were together like this, nothing else mattered. She was overtaken by a strong desire for him and he was the only one who could tame it.

His hands rested on her buttocks, he caressed, loving how her body was in tune with him, it reacted to his every look and touch and sound.

She both hated and loved how he made her feel. She had always possessed self-control but now she wasn't sure of that any longer.

His cock strained painfully in the confines of his pants but tonight wasn't for him, it was for Aryann, to make her know that no man can ever make her feel so good except him.

He moved his hand to her back and slowly started zipping down her gown. She felt goosebumps pop up on her skin as the gown fell on the floor.

He broke away from the kiss and she stepped out from her gown. He hurriedly drew off his tie, then started undoing the buttons of his sleeves, he moved forward, guiding her to the bed, she sank down in a whoosh.

He pulled off his sleeves and quickly undid his belt and stepped out of his trousers, shoes and socks leaving himself clad in only his briefs. He bent before her and took off her bra, he nudged her to lie flat on the bed.

Luca slowly hovered atop her, scattering hot kisses all over her body. He sucked on her neck harshly enjoying the gasps that fell from her mouth. He slid his tongue over the ache to soothe it.

Luca moved downwards kissing the upper slope of her breasts and the furrows between them. He ran his fingers around the rim of her panties then tugged it down her body. Spreading her legs, he gazed at her slick feminine folds as if he was seeing it for the first time.

He lowered his head but felt her body jerked. He lifted up his head, her innocence still amuses him.

"Relax, you'll like this" He assured and bent his head.

"Lu………ca" She gasped feeling his tongue inside her body, his mouth closed and he suckled her deeply.

"Uhmm…..Ahhh" She moaned.

He wanted to tell her how wet she was, how ready but he couldn't find any words, her noises and the her hands gripping the sheet from the pleasure he was giving her consumed him.

He replaced his mouth with one finger, sliding in and out of her as she whimpered. He nibbled her clit making her moan louder.

Aryann was dazed, she never knew anything could feel like this in her entire life, she didn't want this to end.

"Don't stop, please" She begged in a voice that sounded so unlike hers.

She closed her eyes and moaned in ecstasy as his long finger move deeply into her body.

"Open your eyes, I want you to see who's making you feel like this" He demanded.

Slowly, her eyes opened.

"You're beautiful" He whispered.

His words almost blew her mind into irreplaceable pieces.

"I love how your body respond to my touch" He muttered, circling her body, plunging in and out.

"I'm the only one who can make you feel like this" He declared, his eyes never leaving hers.

He pulled out his finger and suckled her again.

She moaned in great pleasure, her body writhing against his face, humping up and down, he noticed her legs stiffening, the way they always do when she's close, he pull back to watch his fingers rub over her nub and folds from side to side.

"Come for me, beautiful" He urged. Within seconds, her orgasm hit her hard.

"Luca!" She screamed as her head pushed back into the pillow and her body trembled from the intensity, waves of pleasure flew through her body.

Chapter four

Luca stared at her as she comes all over his fingers, he looked up to her face, taking in every detail, the way her eyes screwed shut, the way her mouth forms an O, her chest and cheeks flushed a light pink as she goes through her orgasm, she was stirring something inside his chest but he'll never acknowledge it.

He slid his finger into his mouth after she is done. She tasted so good.

He slowly lay down beside her, he glanced at her, her eyes were still closed probably shy to look at him.

He grinned wondering when she'd finally get use to this, he heaved himself up resting on his side then slowly he tucked some loose strands of her hair behinds her ear.

Her eyes shot opened and for a tensed moment, their eyes locked. Luca stared at her eyes, they were so beautiful that he didn't want to look away but when he started having trouble drawing air into his lungs, he quickly looked away.

"You should get some sleep" He muttered.

Aryann gulped, she wanted to ask him why he always stayed in her room after taking her to bed but then she wasn't in any position to ask so she closed her eyes trying her best to fall asleep.

When Luca was sure that she had fallen deeply asleep, he moved closer and covered them with the duvet then he slowly wrapped his arms around her, he couldn't leave, as much as he tried to, he couldn't. He loved it when she's asleep in his arms.

Luca walked into his mansion, he'd had a busy day at work and was so exhausted. As he got closer to the living room, he heard Aryann's voice.

"Logen wasn't at fault for not giving those guys her letters, I think Peter should've been more outspoken" She sounded excited.

"You don't say. Peter was cool, I think the one who was too quiet was Logen" A familiar voice which he immediately recognized to be Harry's replied.

He quickly hastened his footsteps. What the hell was Harry doing in his house?

"Yeah, I get it, you're a guy so you're taking sides with the male lead."

Harry laughed. "I am not, Missy. I'm a fair judge" He said and nudged her playfully. She laughed.

Luca scowled on seeing Harry. Today was his day off but the last place he was expecting to see him was in his house, sitting on his couch beside Aryann and making her laugh!

"What are you doing here?" He asked, coldly.

They turned to look at him surprised.

Harry stood up." Hey Luca, it's nice to see you too" He replied, cheerfully.

"You still haven't answered my question" He reminded with his hands tucked inside his pocket.

Maria walked out from the kitchen, she had loved the way Harry and Aryann got along since noon, he'd been making her laugh a lot, something that rarely happens and she didn't want Luca to end that.

"Oh Luca, the plumber working on Harry's house made a terrible mistake and it won't be fixed till tomorrow so he came here, I hope that isn't a problem."

"It's a big problem, there are many hotels in this city" Luca snapped.

"C'mon, it's been awhile since I came here, I just saw it as a good opportunity to hang out with you" Harry said.

"Hang out with me or Aryann" Luca thought.

"Luca, he's only going to spend the night, please" Maria begged.

Luca stared at Aryann, she was giving him the "bad friend" look.

"Fine" He grunt and strode away.

Harry heaved a sigh of relief.

"That went well!" He exclaimed.

Maria laughed and walked away.

He sat down beside Aryann again.

"How long have you been friends with him?" Aryann asked, curiously.

"Since we were in diapers, you see, my parents were friends with his"

"Woah!I wonder how you could put up with him for so long"

Harry grinned." Well, he can be so self-absorbed but I know he's soft on the inside"

Aryann huffed.

"It's true, you know in high school, Luca used to beat up jerks for my sake, I never got bullied, not that I was weak though but he gets so angry when I'm cornered and he was like,' Get your fucking hands off him" He said mimicking Luca's voice.

Aryann smiled, did Luca really have a soft demeanor?

"His voice is quite intimidating. Are you good at guessing?" Harry asked and stood up.

"A little"

"Well, this wouldn't be hard" And then, he crossed his hands behind him and raised his head up high trying to look tough.

She stared at him, confused.

"Don't give me that look, woman, I'm not an ordinary man" He snapped trying to sound like Luca but fails miserably.

Aryann laughed." I think his voice is deeper than that" She pointed out.

Harry grimaced slightly." I think someone is getting to know him more than I do"

"That's not me" She retorted, quickly.

"Well, for the fact that I'm standing here before you and talking to you, you should consider it a blessing" He said again now sounding like Luca.

Aryann giggled, was she actually happy that they were making fun of Luca?

"Hey woman, I did not permit you to laugh!" Harry shot at her sounding harsh.

Aryann frowned." So if you want to laugh in front of him, you need his permission"

"Well there was this particular day, there had been a heavy downpour of rain, he slipped and fell in front of me, I had laugh so hard and then he said he didn't permit me to laugh" Harry explained.

Aryann grinned wondering how he'd look like on the ground.

"But I knew he was joking when he laughed too" He added.

She wondered how he'd look like if he laughs, she thought she had seen him laugh that night when she tried to seduce him but he was quick to deny it.

"Harry!" Luca's voice sounded in the air startling the two of them, they silently prayed that he heard nothing, he would be furious if he knew that they had been making jest of him.

Harry slowly turned to face him.

"You need to translate some paperwork" He announced.

Harry smirked, he knew Luca was trying to get him away from Aryann.

"This isn't the company and its my day off" He reminded and saw Luca's eye flashed dangerously.

"If you love your job, you'll come with me" He threatened and walked off.

Harry turned to face Aryann.

"I'm going to the land of no return" He said, jokingly.

"And I shall pray for you" Aryann replied bringing her palms together. They laughed and he walked away.

"What were you telling her that made her laugh?" Luca asked as soon as Harry got seated in a chair opposite him in his study.

"Jokes" Harry replied.

"What kind of jokes?" Luca asked, curiously.

Harry laughed uneasily." Jokes that you wouldn't find funny."

Luca frowned but they made her laugh anyway.

"Write them down!" Luca ordered giving Harry a piece of paper and a pen.

"Why?"

"Do I really have to explain myself to you?"

"You wanna make her laugh, don't you?" Harry asked smiling sheepishly.

"No" Luca retorted." I just wanna see if they are indeed funny"

Harry stared at him suspiciously then started writing down some jokes he knew of.

Luca wanted to make her laugh, even if he didn't succeed at that, he wanted her to at least smile…. smile at him. A part of him thought the idea sounded pathetic but he couldn't resist the urge to make her smile.

Harry stretched out the piece of paper to him and stood up to leave.

"And where do you think you're going?" Luca asked.

Harry frowned." The living room"

Luca's jaw tightened, as much as he wanted Aryann to laugh all the time, he didn't want another man eliciting laughter from her.

He threw some files at Harry.

"Translate those!" He ordered.

Harry scoffed and sat right back." Why do I get the feeling that you don't want me to be around Aryann?"

Luca glanced at him." I don't usually like to see any of my past women around you."

"That's a gigantic lie, Luca. You were aware that Kate flirted with me but you weren't even affected, whereas Aryann and I are just getting along as friends but you're getting worked up."

"I am not, you two are just being noisy, that's why I want you here so that my house can be quiet again"

Harry smirked." Alright, so can I go back to her now, I promise to be as………."

"No! keep your ass glue to that chair and translate those files! He thundered.

Harry chuckled shaking his head." She has you bad, Luca" He thought.

Luca stood in the landing of the staircase, from where he stood, he could see Aryann sitting on a couch in the living room reading a book, Harry had left almost an hour ago after breakfast.

He stood there for a while, his mind was conflicted. He was contemplating whether to walk up to her and tell her the jokes he had memorized last night or just walk away. No! he couldn't just walk away ,if he could stay up late memorizing and practicing how to tell her the jokes then he had to tell her and she must laugh cause she should feel honored that he was trying to make her laugh.

He strode towards her.

"Aryann" He called.

Everyone calls her Aryann but when Luca does it, it sounds so intimate and lovely. She ignored the prickling sensation in her cheeks, drew a deep breath and lifted up her head to face him. He was clad in a navy blue suit and black suede shoes. He was like a god, a rakishly handsome god.

"Hmmm" He cleared his throat tucking his hands into his pocket.

"When an almond dies, what does it become?" He asked, seriously.

"Diamond" Aryann replied, flatly.

"What do you call an animal who wears bra?" He asked, sternly.

"Zebra" She replied getting confused as to why he was asking her these jokes.

Luca frowned, this wasn't how it was supposed to go, she's not supposed to know the answers, he was the one to say the answers then she'll laugh.

"What's an apple that isn't an apple?" He pressed on.

"Pineapple" She replied, she had seen these jokes online, at first it amused her but seeing them all the time didn't make them sound funny any more.A thought occurred to her. Why was Luca asking her these jokes?

Luca didn't like the strange look she was giving him.

"I saw those questions somewhere and I was curious to know the answers" He said.

Aryann nodded curtly.

He glanced at her and walked off.

"She didn't laugh!" Luca thundered barging into Harry's office.

Harry sighed." What are you talking about?"

"Don't act dumb with me. You purposely wrote down jokes that were not funny" Luca snapped and angrily sat down, he felt humiliated, after all he did trying to make her laugh, she didn't even smile instead she was giving him the "what's wrong with you?" look.

He was brought back to reality on hearing Harry giggling uncontrollably.

"Who are you laughing at?" He shot at him, fiercely.

"Someone who wanted to see if the jokes are indeed funny…."

"Don't get on my nerves, you've already done enough!" Luca warned.

"Well, I'm not gonna ask why you told her jokes cause you won't tell me the truth anyway." But I didn't do anything, it wasn't my fault that she didn't…….."

"It was your fault" Luca accused.

"Look, sometimes jokes might not be funny but the way a person telling the jokes behaves make it funny"

"I don't get you"

"Let me guess, your hands were tucked into your pockets and you were staring at her as if you were some cold professor while telling her the jokes"

"Go straight to the point" Luca snapped.

"What I'm trying to say is that, you had to gesticulate and act playful" Harry replied. His phone beeped, he picked it up from the table and replied to a text.

Luca imagined himself acting playful and gesticulating, he looked ridiculous, like a clown.

"Not happening" He said but Harry wasn't listening, he was smiling at his cellphone and texting someone.

Luca sighed, what the hell came over him? He was never going to do that again. Somehow, he felt sad that he couldn't even make her smile and the beep sound of Harry's phone wasn't helping matters.

"Who the hell are you texting?"

"Aryann" Harry replied, nonchalantly.

"Ary…… Aryann?" Luca asked in disbelief.
Harry nodded.

"Why are you texting her? Why do you even have her number?"
Harry sighed and gently placed his phone on the table.

"We're friends"

"Why are you friends with her?"

"Cause we have a lot in common, things like reading books and we love the same genre of movies."

Luca gulped.

"You've absolutely nothing in common with her" His subconscious mind mocked.
"Delete her number!" He ordered.
"C'mon man, you don't have to get jealous over nothing, I won't make a move on her" Harry assured.

"I'm not jealous! I just………….. Nevermind"
Harry shook his head." When will you finally tell me what's going on with you? Just admit it!I can sense something already but why won't you acknowledge it?

Luca stood up," I don't know what you're talking about. We should stop talking about Aryann, I have better things to do" With that, he walked away.
Since Harry wasn't going to delete her number, he was going to make her lost contact with him instead.

"Maria, you cheated again!" Aryann exclaimed staring at the chessboard.
"I did not, young lady. It's not my fault that I'm so good at this game" Maria said proudly.

Aryann pout. "I can't believe I couldn't even beat you at all"
"Well, you'll need more lessons from the great Maria"

Aryann chuckled.

Luca walked in.

"Maria, excuse us" He ordered.
Maria sighed then nodded and walked away.

Aryann swallowed, she hoped nothing was wrong this time, she hadn't noticed that he was home already.

"I bought you a new phone" He announced bringing out a small carton.
Luca smirked, this would make her glad.
"I already have a phone" She replied calmly, showing him her cellphone.

"That's nothing compared to this and I want you to dispose that crap, don't even think of transferring anything into this phone" He instructed.

Aryann stared at her cellphone, she had gotten it less than eight months ago, after her former cellphone got spoilt, she knew that there was no way Edward would buy her a phone, the first had been given to her by Wyatt ,her neighbour.

She took up a part time job at a diner, and her first paycheck was used in buying this phone, over the months, she'd been saving so that she could afford an apartment and when she finally had enough money, her plans were shattered.

"I don't mean to be rude by rejecting your kind offer but I really love…….."
Her words were cut off when Luca grabbed her cellphone from her hands and smashed it against the floor then stomped on it.

"Now you don't have a cellphone, you need this" He said, harshly.

Aryann stared at her cellphone ruefully. She looked up to face him as tears threatened.

"I didn't do anything wrong this time, did I? I've done everything you wanted, why can't you just……why…..why can't you just………"Her voice hitched, she couldn't finish that because he might just get more angry. Why couldn't he be less mean?

She swallowed back her tears and stood up, without staring at him, she walked away.

Luca stared at the damaged cellphone in his hand. When she had stared at him with tears filled eyes, It had hurt to breathe. What the hell was wrong with him? The high probability that she might be crying made his heart clenched painfully.

She really didn't do anything wrong. He was being paranoid just because Harry made her laugh but he couldn't, Harry had her number but he didn't. Fine! it was impossible making her laugh but it wasn't impossible getting her number, all he had to do was ask.

He stared at the cellphone he bought for her, who would prefer an old crap over this anyway? He rarely bought anything for his past women, he just had to give them money to get whatever they needed.

He stood up from the bed. Aryann should be glad, she should feel blessed not depressed. The fact that she was going to hate him more than she already did tore at him. What should he do to fix this?

Luca walked into the dinning room, there was no sign of Aryann. He slowly sat down across Maria.

"Where's Aryann?" He asked, calmly.

"When I went up to her room, she said she wasn't hungry" Maria replied." I guess someone is bent on making her feel miserable"

"I'm not" Luca snapped.

Maria sighed and continued eating.

"Isn't it strange if someone prefers something low-priced to something expensive" He asked, curiously.

"What did you do to her, Luca" Maria shot at him, fiercely.

"Christ!" Luca exclaimed." I wasn't talking about her."

"Fine! if you ain't telling me what you did then I'm not answering your question."
Luca sighed, as much as he tried not to care about how she feels, he couldn't. He knew something was wrong with him, he didn't care about any other person but himself, right now, he couldn't stop thinking about her sad face.

"I broke her cellphone" He confessed.

"Why?"

Luca gulped, he certainly couldn't tell her that it was because she had Harry's number.

"Well, I bought her a new one but she wouldn't accept it so I broke the old one"

Maria took a deep breath, she recalled Aryann's phone didn't seem faulty.

"Why did you buy her a new phone?"

"Cause hers looked like an ancient phone" He teased.

"It didn't look old" Maria defended.

"Just tell me what to do"

"As if you'd listen"

"If it makes any sense, I might listen"

"To answer your question, to some people, they find some stuff unique, it's not about how pricey stuff are, it's about how they manage to get them, the joy they felt with that thing, even if they want to get it replaced someday, it should be willing……."

"Maria, go straight to the point" Luca interrupted.

"Replace her cellphone with the exact model and try to transfer everything from the damaged…….."

"What? I'm not doing that! Why will I go through all those shit for her?" Luca cut in, rudely.

Maria sighed." I wasn't expecting you to, anyway."

"I'm getting late for work" And then he stood up and walked away.

Aryann sat on a chair in front of the reading table in her bedroom, she stared at her novels, she was tired of reading them over and over again.

She didn't want to disturb Maria to get her another one, She knew Maria wouldn't mind though but she didn't want to take advantage of the woman's kindness toward her.

She wondered how she'll kill this boredom without her cellphone.

When will Luca finally get tired of her? A sound came from the door, she turned to see Luca walking into her bedroom.

Her fists clenched hating the possibility that he might want to take her to bed. She was angry to think that once he touches her, her common sense might disappear.

"I bought you a cellphone" He began.

Aryann sighed, why was he so bent on giving her a new phone? She might just accept it and dump it inside the closet.

"Thanks" She replied, sarcastically.

Luca's teeth clenched trying to ignore her cold reply. He opened the carton of the cellphone, brought it out and placed it on the table gently.

Her eyes dilated on seeing the phone, it was the exact model of the phone he damaged.

"Just think of it as a replacement for the damaged phone.

I tried to get it fixed but it developed a major fault but they could manage to transfer everything from that cellphone into this one" He explained, he couldn't believe he did this all to make her feel better.

He could still remember the frantic look on the repairman's face, he made sure to transfer everything, he was quite intimidated by Luca's presence and Luca spent the whole time ransacking his brain trying to come up with a perfect deduction on what Aryann was doing to him.

Aryann picked up the phone and unlocked it, everything was really intact, it was like her old phone, she slide into her contacts, all her contacts were intact including Harry's. She came by Luca's name.

Luca could see her staring at his name on the screen.

"I just saved mine and took yours too in case you need to text or call me" He said, flatly.

Aryann frowned wondering if she'll have any reason to call or text him.

"Thank you" She muttered, sincerely, she turned in her seat to face him, she saw him holding a little bag.

"I...em....I noticed you love reading books so I thought you might like this" He said giving it to her.

Aryann gasped on seeing the device inside the bag. An e-reader. She had always wanted to have one. She had desperately wanted to buy one soon.

She smiled happily. It was so thoughtful of him, too thoughtful, it was practically the best gift she had ever received.
"Thank you so much, Luca" She said, smiling broadly.

Luca stared at her in awe, his heart plummeted into his stomach, his blood rushed hot in his veins.

She was smiling…… smiling at him. He just made her smile.

He wanted to see her like this for a long time. He didn't want to feel this way towards her, he wasn't sure if he should be scared of it either.

Aryann could see his gaze flicker to her lips. She started hearing voices inside her head saying" Kiss me….kiss me." She knew it was insane to want him right now but seeing how thoughtful he could be made her long to be in his arms.

"I'll leave you to check it out" He said gesturing at the e-reader then he walked away.

Her heart sank. Her room suddenly felt empty, she didn't quite expect that from him. She stared at the e-reader and smiled. She turned on the device.

On the home screen, there are different tabs, she tapped one of them with her finger, a long list of novels appeared.

She smiled knowing that the night would be spent reading and browsing through Luca's wonderful gift.

Maria grimaced slightly on seeing Aryann walking into the dining room holding a cellphone.

"Morning Maria" She greeted cheerfully and sat down.

"Luca left already" Maria announced.
Aryann sighed, she had wanted to see him this morning, she thought about what colour of suit he'd worn. He always looked so good in suits.

She quickly shook her head, she shouldn't be thinking about him.

"Luca bought me a new phone, it's just like the old one" she said showing the phone to Maria.

Maria gasped." Did he also transfer everything from the old one into this? She asked curiously.

"Yes" Aryann replied.

Maria frowned. Luca had listened to her, for the first time he had taken her advice. That was so unlike Luca.

What was happening to him?

Luca ran a hand through his hair as he headed home.

Her smile!

Her smile had been messing up his head, he couldn't stop thinking about it and he desperately wanted to see it again and again. Did Harry and that Jackass feel this way on seeing her smile

She shouldn't smile publicly again. It was too risky. He couldn't wait to have her in his arms. He had never wanted a woman this much, he had never been so impatient to see any woman at the end of the day. How could he possibly let go of her someday?

The car came to a halt, he tilted his head but didn't see any traffic lights.
"Ralph, why are we stopping? He asked the driver.

"There's a fatal accident ahead sir, and it's causing an hold up in traffic"
Luca sighed, the vehicle in front of his car carefully rode around a U-turn taking another route. And from where he sat, he saw a little boy and a woman probably his mother laying lifelessly on a stretcher and being rode into an ambulance.

"We can't seriously have this conversation in front of our kid, Xavier" Megan warned.

"Shut the fuck up and listen to me. I'm so pissed right now and all I can think of is you seeing him again, you promised never to do that again, It's only being one week" Xavier yelled.
"I didn't do anything…….."

"He texted you last night, he told you to meet up with him today, why can't you just look only at me? What have I done to deserve this, I'm sick and tired of sharing your body with other men"
"Xavier……"

"When we get to my parents house, we are gonna tell them that we are getting a divorce"

"You can't do that……."
"I can do anything, I'm nobody's fool!
"You know what, Xavier, I'm tired of this marriage too, you and I know that I never wanted to get married in the first place, it's not my fault that there are other men better than you" Megan yelled.

Luca stared at his parents, he wished they could stop arguing and he desperately wished he had earphones or something so he wouldn't have to listen to all of this.
Xavier turned to face her." You said you loved me, you agreed to marry me because you claimed to love me, you're sick if you think I forced you to. No one did, and it's not my fault that you're a bloody whore!" And then, he revved the car into another route.

Luca's eyes dilated on seeing an incoming truck.
"Dad" He called.

"XAVIER!" Megan screamed and before he could step on his brakes or do anything, a crushing sound was heard and everything went black.

Luca swallowed the thick lump on his throat and slowly lifted up his head again, blood littered the ground. It must have been this way that day, his blood and that of his parents must've littered the ground too, people gathering, some taking pictures and others trying to come up with a tangible deduction as to the cause of the accident.

Pain choked him." Take another route, just get the hell out of here!" He ordered trying to pull himself together.

Aryann quickly tidied up the kitchen, Maria had gone to visit a sick relative so she had to make dinner, Luca had arrived home about thirty minutes ago, he had seem so upset, he didn't even glance at her.

She pulled off her hand gloves and took off her apron, she had to tell him that dinner was ready even if he might not want to eat. As she walked out of the kitchen, a loud sound came from the study. She gulped and slowly walked towards there, she shakily opened the door and peered inside, she could see some broken glasses on the floor. His back was to her.

Aryann gasped as he brushed away everything on the table including his computer which came crashing on the hard floor.

His fists clenched on the table, he was burning with rage but he wanted the feeling to stop, he wanted this rage in his heart to stop. A woman turned his father into a moron. He became a drunk, he became miserable and turned his son into a punching bag.

Even so, Luca had never wanted to grow up an orphan, his parents didn't deserve to die like that and he didn't deserve to go through all those migraines after waking up from coma. At some point, when he saw how happy a kid was with his/her parents. It had made him wished he died too.

Luca felt the presence of someone, abruptly, he turned around to see her standing by the door, he didn't want her to see him like this, his chest ached knowing she would become more scared of him now. He had to say something…… just anything to make her run away from him.

"Go away! I don't wanna hurt you" He warned, frantically.

Chapter five

"I'm not a monster so don't run away from me again."

His words reeled through her mind.
'He won't hurt me, he isn't a monster 'She thought

Her eyes darted to his left hand, his knuckles were bleeding.

"Are you okay?" She asked.

Luca stared at his hand, he didn't realize that he had punched the wall so hard, he lifted up his head to see her walking up to him, why wasn't she running away from him? Wasn't she scared?
She held his hand." It looks bad, will you let me treat your wound?" She asked, timidly meeting his gaze, his features had suddenly softened.

It was like a cold finger touching his heart, his rage was quickly fading.

He simply nodded.

She led him out of the study and hurriedly rushed to search the living room cabinets, the dinning room and kitchen.

Luca stared at her confused as she searched through the lobby.
"I can't find the first aid box" She announced, exhausted.

"I have one in my bedroom" He replied.
'His bedroom. 'Aryann thought.
"I thought……."
"I don't have any rule against that" He cut in, softly.
Damn! He just denied his rule.

Seconds later found them in his bedroom, he was sitting on the bed while she looked around his bedroom astonished at the space, his king size bed, the paintings……

"If you're done looking around, the first aid kit is right there" He said snapping her out of her thoughts.

"Sorry" She apologized and walked up to the drawer that he was pointing at, she brought out the first aid kit and stood before him taking his hand in hers.

As she treated his wound, he stared at her, every little thing about her amuses him, he watched as she absently tucked some loose strands of her hair behind her ear, he watched as she blew air into his wound, he watched as her eyebrows arched together, he wondered what she was thinking about.

"Doesn't it hurt?" She asked wrapping his knuckles with a bandage.
"No" He replied, calmly.

Aryann frowned, it really looked bad or was he pretending. She pressed his knuckles and he flinched.
"What's wrong with you?" He asked, staring at his hand.

Aryann bit her bottom lip trying not to laugh at him.

"You said it doesn't hurt" She reminded, and he could sense mockery in her voice. He love the fact that she was starting to feel free with him.
"It doesn't hurt but don't touch my hand again" He warned.

An awkward silence fell between them, Luca wanted to tell her about his parents but he didn't know where to begin.

Aryann somehow wanted to make him feel better, she was tired of seeing him angry all the time but then she didn't bother to ask herself what it would do to her if she gets to know the other side of him.

"Are you hungry?" She asked.
"No" He released a breath he had been holding." I saw an accident scene today, it always reminds me of my parents"

Aryann stared at him sadly, she couldn't imagine how he must feel right now, how he must have felt waking up from coma and being told that his parents were no more. She desperately wanted to make him feel better. She moved closer to him, standing between his legs, then she wrapped her arms around him making his head rest on her stomach, She didn't want to open old wounds so she didn't ask any questions, She was glad he told her what made him angry.

Luca wrapped his arms around her waist, feeling her delicate body against his made him feel so light-headed. He felt her fingers running through his hair, he smiled. He never knew that it was this possible to be this peaceful, he wanted to be like this with her, he wanted to be with her from dusk till dawn.

"Sleep here tonight" He said, his cheek against her stomach.

"I…. I can't sleep in this" She replied, calmly.

He moved back from her body and stared at her tank top and body-fitted Jean. She really couldn't sleep in this but she might pretend to fall asleep if she goes back to her bedroom.

"You can look for something to wear in there" He said pointing at a door.
Aryann nodded and walked away.

She walked into the dressing room, she opened a closet, she was amazed by the number of suits neatly hanged, she closed the closet and stared at his watches, was he selling them? She came by a shoe rack and shook her head, how can he wear all these in a lifetime?

She opened another closet and found some casual wears.

She brought out a blue t-shirt and brought it up to her nose inhaling his wonderful scent.

Aryann took off her clothes, leaving herself in just her panties then she wore his t-shirt, it was incredibly big and long, reaching her mid thigh, she knew instantly that his shorts wouldn't fit at all. She stared at her reflection on the mirror and smiled. Luca might think that she looked ridiculous but she loved his shirt on her body.

She walked out of the dressing room to find Luca clad in only his briefs, he was sitting on the edge of the bed and busy with his cellphone. Her lips parted at the sight of his chest, ridges of muscles went down his stomach to his waist line.
He lifted up his head, he stared at her intently then he smiled." I like you in my shirt" He confessed.

"I like it too" She thought enchanted against her will by the smile that lit up his face.

He placed his phone on the bedside table and tapped on the other side of the bed. She walked closer to him and slowly lay on the bed, Luca lay down too, covering them with the duvet. He slowly lay on his side propping himself slightly up with his elbow.

"Weren't you scared of me?" Didn't you think I might hurt you?" He suddenly asked.

Aryann turned her head to face him.
"I just wanted to believe that you wouldn't hurt me, you're not a monster"
And those words gladdened his heart, he kept on staring at her, even when she looked away, she could still sense that he was all eyes on her and the intensity of his gaze was becoming unbearable. She turned to face him again.

"Do I have something on my face?"
"No, I just can't keep my eyes off you, do you know how beautiful you are when you're asleep in my arms?" He asked, seriously.

Aryann's heart raced, a warning went off, she didn't like the feelings he was starting to create in her.

"Can't you be less pretty?"

A strange feeling erupted in her stomach and she smiled.

"Stop flattering me, Luca" She thought.
He reached for her and she went to him, allowing herself to be wrapped in his powerful arms, he held her as though she was as precious as his life.

Framing her face between his palms, he dipped his head until his lips grazed hers.

"You should smile all the time, Aryann. I hate seeing your tears"

Her heart melted, was it okay to feel this way?

His thumb flexed on her cheeks ,his eyes grew dark, she was beginning to get used to the waves of aching weakness she experienced whenever he touched her.

Luca stared at her deep red cheeks, he enjoyed making her blush, he hadn't felt this light headed in ages.

"Your cheeks are flaming up" He teased.
Aryann didn't want him to know that his words were affecting her mercilessly.

"It's…… it's hot in here" She stuttered.

Luca slung her a wicked grin full of sexuality and fantasy, his dark golden eyes dancing with amusement and hot pink drenched her cheeks again.

"Am I making you feel hot cause I can also feel the heat, you know."

Aryann averted her gaze, why wouldn't he stop talking? All of a sudden, she didn't want him to get tired of her, at least not so soon. She wanted to lie in bed with him like this again and again.

He had made her feel incredible pleasure that she never knew existed.

She wanted him to feel that way too.

What do men like? Her eyes darted down his body then back at his face.

"What?" Luca asked noticing she seem lost in thoughts.

"Can…… can I touch you?" She asked faintly that he had to strain to hear.
Aryann stared at him, he seem taken aback.

"You wanna touch me?"
She nodded.

"Are you sure?" He asked, teasingly and she nodded again.

He grinned and tossed aside the duvet.
"Let's see what you can do to me"
She slowly crawled between his legs and tugged down her boxer.

Aryann fingers closed around him and he let out be a sharp breath.

she sighed deeply recalling that Nicole had once said it was like licking a lollipop, she had found it disgusting then but now that she was able to do it, now that she wanted to please him, she didn't find it disgusting at all

He was as hard as a rock on her palm, she stroked him and he groaned, slowly she started to caress him teasing him with slow movement.

"Fuck!" He hissed.

She lowered her luscious mouth and sucked his cock. Luca shot his eyes as the dampness of her mouth enveloped him.
When he looked down at her, he felt wild seeing her working her tongue on him, swirling and flicking.

"Ary…. Aryann!" He groaned.

She sucked him harder gritting her teeth along gently, taking more of him into her sweet mouth. It was the prettiest thing he had ever seen, his cock sliding in and out of her beautiful mouth.

He drifted his hand and ran it through her swollen lips, she lifted her head slightly and he groaned at the image of his cock in her mouth.

His head fell back into the pillow as she took him in deeply.

"Mmmmm" He moaned as his hips jerked, she bobbed her mouth up and down, increasing her assault on his manhood, bringing him closer and closer.

The feeling was indescribable and he was helpless to move, he wanted to run his hands through her hair but felt his power being drained out of him.

The combination of her mouth on his cock and her fingers rubbing him was the most intensed sensation he'd ever experienced.

As his orgasm started to crash through him, she took her mouth away and stared at him, his chest rising and falling like a tandem as he comes into his stomach.

Luca tried to steady his breath as the most thrilling climax he had ever experience subsided.

He weakly sat up.

"What the hell was that?" He gasped.
Her face flushed quite embarrassed, she knew she did a bad job.

"I'll get cleaned up" With that, he stood up and walked into the bathroom.

Aryann quickly lay down, she needed to be fast asleep, she couldn't face him knowing that she couldn't be an equal bed partner.

Minutes later, he walked back into the bedroom, she had covered herself with the duvet, he knew she was pretending to be asleep.

He grinned and lay beside her.

"That was….. you know……"He trailed off unable to find the right word for it.
She slowly opened her eyes." Please don't laugh at me"

"What do you mean? it was incredible, I haven't felt that way before" He confessed.

Aryann smiled." I haven't done that before" She reminded.

Pride puffed up his chest, he was happy that he was the only one who had seen all of her.

"I don't want you to feel bad about it, I'm glad I was your first time" He smiled seeing her cheeks flushed again.

He moved closer to her and kissed her forehead then made her lay spawl over his chest. Aryann burried her face into his neck.

Things were spiraling out of control and when he would finally let go of her, she knew that it'd hurt…….it'd hurt a lot.

The morning sun woke Aryann up,she opened her eyes and saw Luca staring down at her. Not today again, she couldn't take it if he starts his soft demeanor again and at the same time,she didn't want the frosty Luca.

He smiled." Good morning"
She slowly sat up."Good morning" She replied.
"Take a shower with me" He offered.
Aryann frozed. A shower with Luca? That was too intimate.
"I don't like……"

"Don't act shy with me when last night you sucked my……."
She quickly covered his lips with her palm.

"You don't have to remind me"
She felt him chuckled against her palm, her heart warmed, she quickly took her hand away.

He moved closer to her and kissed her with a slow, deep hunger that made her heart crash against her breastbone.

Luca took his lips away and ran a hand through her cheeks as if he couldn't help touching her, he still found her both seductive and innocent after waking up.
"So, will you take a shower with me?" He asked in a seductively husky voice.
How could she say no when between her thighs was pulsing with desire.

She nodded and he quickly carried her in his arms. At that moment, she felt special.
In what felt like seconds, he was in the bathroom, he gently lower her down till she was standing.

He turned on the shower.

Aryann stared at his body as he slowly took off his briefs, She stared at the water streaming down his chest to his abs…….

"Should I keep standing here so you can admire my body for a long time?"
"Yes" She replied absentmindedly then he brain registered what he said.
"No, I wasn't admiring your body, I was just thinking about something else" She added, quickly

Luca shrugged and watched her take off his shirt and her panties.

He moved closer and ran his hand through her body, down her hips.

"I can't seem to get used to seeing this" And then he took her lips with his, bringing a hand to her hair, spearing through it, massaging her skull.

His mouth moved over hers with expect precision, teasing and tasting.

He moved back staring at her eyes, his body was going up in flames and she was the only person that was capable of assuaging it.

Their lips locked again and
they moved until her back was against the wall.

Rush of sensation made her legs feel weak.

She was crippled by his touch.

Her lips parted and Luca uttered a groan deep in his throat.

His hands left her head to descend all over her body and then he hauled her into his lean length.

When his tongue touched hers, Aryann heard a mewl coming out from her throat, Luca thrust one hard thigh between her legs and she felt an explosion of hot, wet lust at her core.

His hand moved up over the curve of her waist and cupped one breast, his thumb brush over her nipple, he moved his hips and she felt his burgeoning arousal.

Her arms were already around his neck, her legs felt wobbly and she wanted to press every inch of her body into his.

Flames of passion was escalating so fast as the kiss grew hotter and heavier in seconds.

Luca tore his mouth away, breathing harshly, with his next move, he turned her away so that her back was to his chest.

He kissed her bare back sending delicious thrill over her skin.

She felt distracted by the bulge of his arousal against her buttocks.

The familiar melting sensation started up in her belly, the tips of her breasts tingled. She slowly led his hand to her breasts.

It was like taking a handful of glory, they were soft and firm.

Her breasts tightened against his fingers, her nipples rose tautly and his fingers became entangled between them. He squeezed gently.
"Hmmmm" She breathed, resting her head on his collar bone.

Bending her a little, he grasped his cock in his hand and teased her entrance with the tip. Slowly, he slid inside, stretching her with his thickness, his length, claiming her fully.

They moaned and he pulled out and thrust in again.

"Fuck!" He groaned.

He pounded into her roughly and she screamed.

"Do you like this? Do you like my cock slamming in and out of you!" He asked, hoarsely, thrusting in and out of her relentlessly.

"Oh……Yes!" She moaned.

Hearing her admit to it consumed him with pride and he deepened his thrust.

He gasped at the sensation the position brought and kissed and nipped up and down her shoulders and neck.

"You feel so good around me" He groaned into her neck.

She moaned loudly. His movement became harder, faster.

His world narrowed to the reality of their bodies joining, a place of sharp Bliss and swirling sensation.

Their bodies were soaked with cool water.

He continued gliding into her, turning inside out. Her body came sliding up and down the slick wall.

Taking her hand in his, he laced their fingers together and moved them down her body to her clit, both hands, stroking and teasing.

She gasped as the feeling threatened to overtake her. She was tightening around him, her breaths were coming quickly.

"LUCA!" She yelped as her orgasm hit her hard. He closed his eyes and let the waves overtake him. His final thrust was deep and hard

She dimly felt a warm release inside of her.

Aryann leaned back into him and he steadied himself, both finding it hard to regain their equilibrium. They stood there quietly for a few minutes hearing only their breaths that was slowly becoming normal.

He back hugged her and kissed her neck.

"I'm going on a business trip to France for one week. If you need to get anything, Maria would see to it"He whispered.

Aryann sighed deeply. A week without Luca would surely make her realize that it was the sex she was getting to love and not him.

It has been two long days and he hasn't even called. Who does that?

Aryann thought angrily taking her bath and thinking of when they had showered together, he had practically soaped and washed her body and when he had washed her hair, she felt like she was in the seventh heavens.

God! Why was Luca acting like this?
His arrogant gaze.

His somewhat harsh way of speaking.
Was that what was shaking her heart?
No! Luca should stop invading her mind. She wasn't even safe in her dreams, he wouldn't stop appearing.

"You miss him" Her subconscious mind echoed in her head.
"I don't" Aryann argued.

Why would she miss him? She was happy that he was away. She was happy that he didn't call.

Aryann walked into the kitchen.

"Alright then, take care of yourself" She heard Maria say to someone on the phone. She hung up and turned around.
"Oh! Hello dear" Maria smiled.
Aryann grinned.

"That was Luca, he wanted to check up on you"

Her smile widened." Really?"
"Yes"

"How is he? Did he sound okay? She asked without thinking then she noticed Maria staring at her strangely.

"I'm just asking" Aryann shrugged.
"He seem okay"
"Oh….. okay" She replied trying to sound nonchalant.

"Would you like to go grocery shopping with me? I just wouldn't be comfortable knowing that you're alone in this house"
Luca didn't want her to go anywhere without his permission. As if reading her thoughts, Maria spoke." Luca wouldn't mind, now go get dressed

Aryann nodded, she really couldn't stay in this house alone when her heart was in a roller coaster of feelings and emotions.

Was it just her or was Aryann acting strange today?

Maria stared at the trolley, Aryann had been putting everything Luca loves eating into it.

What about her? Wasn't Aryann gonna put what she loves into it?
"Aryann?" Someone called, they both turned around to see Nicole.

Aryann frozed seeing Nicole holding a shopping basket. Nicole only went shopping for clothes, shoes and bags.

Nicole stared at her, stunned. It had always made her angry that Aryann was too beautiful.

She had expected to see a depressed and shattered looking Aryann after being sent to live with a heartless billionaire.

But here, she was clad in floral shorts and an emerald green t-shirt, her brown hair was neatly packed in a ponytail. She was glowing….

"Nicole, how's Mom? Aryann asked unable to figure out the right words to say

"She's fine and I'm glad to see you"
Glad? Nicole?

"Well, I have to get going now, it was nice seeing you" And then, she walked away.
"That was awkward and she didn't look glad seeing you!" Maria exclaimed.

Aryann grinned." Don't tell me about it"

Luca stared at his laptop, he was sitting on the bed in his suite.

Her face popped into his head.

He shut his laptop, things were getting out of hand and being away from her was worsening issues.

He stared at his cellphone, he didn't want to call Maria again, Maria's voice wasn't the voice he desperately wanted to listen to. There was no big deal in calling Aryann, right? Without thinking twice, he dailed her number.

Aryann stared at the caller's ID on her cellphone and her heart stopped, he was calling, she should pick up? No! She didn't want to pick up right away, he would think that she had been waiting for his call.
When she finally decided to pick up, he rang off.

Her heart fell, she should have answered the call sooner, wouldn't he call again? should she call? No! she shouldn't, there was no big deal in not answering his…….
Her phone rang, seeing it was Luca, she quickly picked up.

"What took you so long?" He asked, calmly.

"I was at the bathroom"
"Oh!" He bit out trying to will himself not to think about her unclad body in the bathroom.
"How are you?"
"I'm fine"

"I hope you didn't miss any of your meals" He asked, concerned.
"I didn't"

An awkward silence set in between them, he was at a loss for words.
"Tell me how your day went" She requested.

"Nah. You'll probably get bored listening to the seminars and meeting up with an investor. Why don't you tell me how your day went?"
"I……."

"Let me guess, you read books and watched movies" He cut in, softly.
He heard her chuckle and wished he could see her face.

"Do you like novels?"
'I hate novels' He thought.
"I love novels" He replied.

"Well then, let's talk about our views on Jess promise" She suggested.
Jess…. what?

"I haven't read that novel"
"What about Wyatt's ready made family?"

"I have forgotten what I read about that book"
Aryann frowned." You haven't read any novel"

He had just been caught. What the hell did he have in common with her, anyway?

"No, but I'll like to listen to the ones you read today"

"Really?" She asked, excitedly.
"Yeah"

And she started talking, he loved the excitement in her voice, he didn't even know she was talking about different novels, he couldn't even remember the titles. He just wanted to hear her voice, it was making him feel relaxed.

He didn't know how long they were on the phone but when it was time to hang up, he was reluctant. After finally wishing her good night, he hung up.
Aryann smiled at her cellphone, it was nice talking to him. He phone beeped, it was a text from Luca.
'I permit you to dream of me'
Heat warmed her cheeks.' Good night, Luca'

Luca grinned staring at her text, when he finally fell asleep, there was half a smile on his face.
"You can't do this to me, the banks are refusing to grant me a loan and if I don't pay back the former loan, they are going to kick me out of my home, please, you have to help me"
Edward pleaded to one of his business Partners but the line went dead.

"Damn it!" He exclaimed as his fists clenched around his cellphone.

He had just lost a contract worth half a billion. He had practically invested all his money into it. Susan did warn him of the risk involved though but he had only thought about the positive side. All his workers were gradually resigning, he could no longer pay them.

He strode into the dinning room and met Susan setting the table, Nicole was already seated.

"Nicole, you didn't buy enough beef" Susan said.

Edward sat down.

"The money dad gave me wasn't enough" She reminded.

Edward sighed.
"Oh! That reminds me, I saw Aryann yesterday at the grocery store"
"She looked miserable, doesn't she?"

"Well, that was how I expected her to look when I see her again but she looked okay, she was more than okay and you needed to see the expensive clothes on her body, I had seen them online and………"

"You mean Aryann is doing perfectly fine" Edward cut in.

"Yeah, I guess Luca is showering her with gifts and money" Nicole replied.

Edward teeth clenched.

If he had known that Luca wasn't that ruthless, he would've given Nicole to him, Nicole would've saved him from this mess.

"Well, let's not judge a book by its cover, none of us have been to his house so we don't know what she might've been through" Susan said.

Edward smirked. Aryann was with Luca because of the choices he made. She had to save him from this mess. She was born to always help him out.

"Oh please Susan! Don't act like a saint, she's doing okay and she's gonna help me, all I need is a perfect plan and time and I'll have her wrapped around my fingers again!"

Chapter six

"One more day to go and we'll be back home, I can't wait" Harry said slumping on a chair in the bar stand, he was sitting beside Luca in a restaurant.

Luca stared at his wine glass, the memory of the of them lying in bed, simply holding each other lingered in his head, he couldn't wait to make her wear his shirt again.

He thought about her smile and how hard he had made her blush.
He smiled broadly.

"And what's Almighty Luca thinking about?" Harry asked.
"Nothing!"

"Really? you were smiling but I didn't say anything about funny"
"Can't you mind your business for once."
Harry shrugged." I can't. Especially not now when you're falling for someone"
"I'm not falling for Aryann!" He retorted quickly.

"See, I didn't even mention her name. The signs are already there Luca, you get mad seeing another man staring at her, you feel bittered just with the thought that she might be thinking about someone else not you, right?"

"That's gibberish, I don't care about that ,I don't care about how she feels"
Harry sighed." You wanna make her happy, you wanna hear her voice all the time, you think of her every damn time, you don't want to see her tears" He pressed on.

"What makes you so sure of what you're talking about?"
"Let's just say I know you more than you know yourself. You're falling in love with her Luca, Why do you keep on denying this? What are you scared of? I know this is new to you but do you think you can turn those feelings off?"

Luca swallowed. Was this really love that he felt for Aryann? Why couldn't it be just sex?
"You're messing up my life, you're ruining me and I hate you for that, just get tired of me already"
Her words reeled through his mind and his chest ached.

He had always despised some of his past women for becoming too attached to him. Now, he despised himself terribly, for becoming too attached to Aryann. She was like a drug that he was desperately addicted to. He had to turn this feelings off. He didn't want to jump into anything, he didn't want to have his hopes up. She didn't feel this way and he shouldn't either.

"I admit, she's different from the rest but I don't love her, soon, I'm gonna let go of her and then replace her!" He said smoothly.

'smooth talkers are great liars' Harry thought.

"Well, you know where to find me, I'm just giving you a few days and you'll run to me for help" He assured.

Luca laughed uneasily "Dream on"

Aryann nearly choked on her glass of milk when Luca strode into the house looking disheveled and unshaven.

Has it only been one week? He looked gorgeous in his grey suits.

Luca stared at her, he needed to think straight but She was driving every rational thoughts from his head, why has she gotten more beautiful? He should just bid her good night since it was late anyway.

"How was your trip?" She asked.

"It was okay I guess. Is Maria in bed already?"

"Yeah"

"Well, I'm tired so I have to retire to bed now" And then, he turned around.

Aryann sighed, they were back to his cold demeanor again. She couldn't believe that this was the Luca she had been talking to on the phone.

"I missed you" She confessed without thinking.

He stopped dead in his tracks, she shouldn't have said that, it had broken the last thin wall safeguarding his heart.

He turned around and hurried towards her. He hauled her into his arms and within seconds, he was kissing her with a hot, driving hunger that left her dizzy with its intensity. Her body quickened, desire rising embarrassingly fast so that she pushed against his hard muscular frame, her breath ragged in her throat, her nipples tight and throbbing.

"Bed" Luca muttered thickly, grasping her hand and urging her out of the room and up the stairs.

"I thought you were ti……"

He cut her off with another kiss, the hunger he roused in her with the second kiss was fierce and relentless, every plunge of his tongue sending a responsive quiver through her slight body.

They had barely made it to door of his bedroom, still fully clothed, they were enjoying each other up against a wall with a scorching raw-edged passion that Luca had never dared to unleash on a woman before.

They staggered into his bedroom and he kicked the door closed.

It was as if there were flames desperate for fuel burning in her heart as she hauled off his jacket and pulled opened his shirt. He laughed softly and then crushed her mouth almost savagely beneath his. As he removed her clothes with impatient hands, she knew that, somehow, the same overwhelming urgency and need for fulfilment was driving him.

They sank into his bed, there was no mistaking the expression in his eyes, he wanted her desperately.

"Unbind your hair" He said, hoarsely.

Wordlessly, she obeyed and pulled off her ribbon, her hair tumbled around her shoulders. Reverently, Luca sifted his fingers through the heavy strands. Then he dipped his head and kissed the valley between her breasts, her scent intoxicated him. He trailed his tongue to one nipple and drew it into his mouth.

She gasped as he suckled, scraping his teeth gently.

"I missed you" He murmured.

'He missed having sex with you' A voice echoed in her head.

Her heart squeezed but she quickly shook it off, maybe this was what she missed too...... having sex with him.

Aryann threaded her fingers through his hair as his lips journeyed to her stomach. He pressed his open mouth over her navel, swirling his tongue in the indentation and causing her hips to arch off the bed.

He kissed a path to her clitoris. Her womb clenched and her thighs went slick. All thoughts, all questions fled. She wanted to feel him inside her body.

He licked lower on her body, his lips sliding to the slick folds at the entrance of her body, he delved deep with his tongue.

"Uhmm....Luca" She moaned, her hips lifted, silently pleading.

He shoved himself off the bed just long enough to rid himself of the rest of his clothes.

When he mounted the mattress again, she pressed him down and crawled over him, dipping her head and lapping at his skin with her tongue. He tasted salty. She licked him again, her tongue traveling over his flesh with a long, erotic slide.

He groaned. Hands bracketing her hips, he lifted her and positioned the entrance to her body at the tip of his erection. With a wrenching sigh, she impaled herself on his rigid shaft, taking him in inch by inch until he was fully embedded inside her. Her inner muscles clenched, holding him safe as he moved inside her, her moans encouraging every upward thrust of his hips. His breathing was harsh, his skin slick.

Her head fell back as she rode him, he sucked in a breath as her hair brush against his thighs.

She couldn't hold back, didn't want to. He was so hard inside her, stroked her so deeply. Her climax crashed like a tsunami. Luca groaned out her name at the same time. She convulsed atop him, her head coming to forward to press into the hollow of his shoulder. His breathing was labored. She could feel his heart pounding against her chest.

He soothed his hand over her shoulders, her back. When she lifted her head, he tucked some strands of her hair behind her ear and smiled. Their gazes locked for long moments. Finally, he looked away.

"Did you leave the house when I was in France?" He asked calmly.

Aryann frozed, Maria had said that he wouldn't mind.

"Yes"

She could feel his body tensed beneath hers.

"Where did you go to?" He asked trying not to lose his temper, he just hope she didn't go to see that Cole guy.

"You have to promise me that you won't get mad, please" She pleaded.

Luca's teeth clenched, Was it that bad?

"I won't" He choked out.

"I went grocery shopping with Maria" She confessed.

Relief washed over him. It was just that? He noticed the fear in her voice. No! He didn't want her to be scared of him.

"I'm……. I'm sorry for locking you up in the basement, no matter what you do, it won't happen again" He said, remorsefully.

Aryann smiled.

Luca slowly held her hand.

"So am I forgiven?"

Aryann nodded.

He slowly moved her off his body and stood up, he wore his boxer and she watched as he disappeared into the dressing room.

Seconds later, he came back holding a black t-shirt, he gave it to her.

"I think I can sleep soundly if you're wearing my shirt" He said lying beside her while she tried hard not to blush as she put on his shirt.

He held her hand and made her rest her head on his chest.

"Luca" She called.

"Hmmm"

"Did you really threaten to kill me and my family?" She asked, curiously.

Luca knew he had to be truthful, he didn't want to give her any more reasons to be scared of him.

"I didn't but I wanted to wreck down the house. Edward didn't keep to his word so I was mad"

"But your men always carry guns about"

"Well, at first I had gotten those guns for protection when I almost got assasinated by a business rival of mine, but over the years, I started using it to intimidate people who think they could step on me"

Luca bit his lower lip, he wished she wouldn't judge him harshly.

"But I swear, my men have never killed any innocent person before" He added.

Aryann sighed, she believed him, she had no reason to doubt him. It occur to her that Susan had said that to make sure she agrees to go with Luca but now, she wasn't sad about it.

"Tell me about Paris" She suggested, changing the topic.

Luca grinned, he figured she hasn't been there before, he suddenly wanted to take her there someday.

"Well, you need to be very fluent in French so as to be able to communicate with most people there"

Aryann nodded." How do you say, I want to eat in French?" She asked, curiously.

"Tu es beau!" He replied.

"Tu es beau!" She repeated.

"Thank you"

"Why are you thanking me?" She asked, confused.

"You said I'm handsome" He replied, laughing.

Aryann smacked his hand, playfully.

"You tricked me!" She exclaimed and laughed too.

Luca's heart fluttered.

"So should I answer your question now?"

"How sure am I that you won't deceive me again?"

"C'mon, I won't.

Embrasse-moi!, now say it" He said.

"Embrasse-moi!" She replied.

"With pleasure" And then, he lifted up her chin, bent his head and kissed her passionately.

"That doesn't mean I want to eat, does it?" She asked, breathlessly.

Luca chuckled." No, It meant Kiss me"

"I'm not repeating anything you say again" She declared and rested her head on his chest again.

"Tu me manques ,ma Belle !"He drawled.

"And what does that mean?" Aryann asked, curiously.

"I missed you, beautiful one" He said, softly.

She felt butterflies letting loose in her belly, a warm rise of blush flamed her cheeks and she knew she couldn't keep on listening to him tonight, She quickly drew the duvet over her body.

"Good night, Luca" She muttered, trying to will herself to fall asleep.

He pressed a kiss to her forehead.

"Good night"

About two hours later, he was still awake, she had fallen deeply asleep but he couldn't sleep, Harry's questions ran through his head. Aryann had stolen his heart and there was no way he could get it back, he was completely at the mercy of someone nearly half his size.

Admitting that sent shrills running down his spine. His heart raced. He slowly moved away from her careful not to wake her up then he sat on the edge of the bed and burried his head into his palms.

He thought about the many times he had made her cry, when she got into his car at her family's house, when he had deflowered her, locking her up in the basement, that night at the party, when she had ran away from him, smashing her cellphone.

Everything he had done to her hurt. He knew she was more comfortable around him and she enjoyed each time they made love. Yes! that was it, they weren't just having sex, they were making love. He had been making love to her. Did she see him differently now? Did she want to be with him willingly? He knew he didn't deserve anything from her but it hurts to know that he was the only one who felt this way.

He slowly turned around to see her sleeping peacefully.

"I can't let you go, Aryann, I've fallen in love with you"

Harry walked into Luca's office, he slowly sat on the visitor's chair opposite an obviously disturbed Luca.

"You sent for me" He began.

Luca ran a hand through his hair." I won't beat around the bush, I just wanted to tell you that you were right" He admitted, ruefully.

"Right? As in?"

"I've fallen for her" He confessed.

Harry smiled, triumphantly." So did you tell her?"

Luca frozed." Tell her? Not happening"

"She needs to know"

"She doesn't need to know"

"Why?"

"Cause she's gonna see me as…….you know……I just…..fuck!" He exclaimed, frantically.

"You're scared of what her reply would be"

Luca sighed." Yes. No matter how hard I try, I can't turn this feelings off, it keeps getting stronger each time I see her…….She hates me. I don't know how much though, but she said I was ruining her life. How am I supposed to tell her that I can't let her go, how am I supposed to tell her that I love her, she might not even believe me"

Harry stared at him for a while, he couldn't believe that this was the same Luca who had been so cold towards people, who didn't care about anyone. Who would have thought that someone like Aryann would make him this desperate?

"Stop looking at me like that, I know I seem desperate right now but you don't have to remind me"

"It's okay to feel this way, Luca. And I like Aryann."

On seeing Luca's angry eyes, he quickly added." I mean, I like her for you. You've got to take it easy, bro" Harry laughed.

"Do you want her to love or let's say like you"

"Is that even possible, when I think about all the things I've done to her……"

"Luca, you need to stop being hard on yourself, I'm not saying what you did was right, but if you keep thinking about it, it'll only break you apart. Did you apologized?"

"Well, not for everything though"

"You hardly apologize for anything, this is getting intensed" Harry smirked.

"Will you just shut up and help me?"

"If you're gonna act bossy, I won't help you"

"Are you threatening me?"

"C'mon, I have to act bossy at times, you know" Harry joked but Luca didn't laugh.

He cleared his throat." So will you do everything I tell you to do?"

"If it makes any sense........."

"It doesn't have to make sense, Luca. You just have to do it if you want Aryann to feel something for you too"

"Fine, so what should I do?"

"First, you need to stop glaring at people all the time, your eyes might give her a heart attack"

Luca frowned." What's wrong with my eyes?"

"I don't know, but most time, when I see you in the morning ,the way you look at me always make me think I shot you in your dream the previous night" Harry chortled.

Luca rolled his eyes." There's nothing wrong with my eyes and for your information, she's now comfortable around me" He said, proudly.

Harry laughed," You're speaking like someone who just won a prize beyond price"

Luca grinned, Aryann was priceless but she wasn't his fully." So, can you proceed?"

"Sure, sir Luca. Next is your temper, if anything is bothering you, don't break anything, please. Just look for a quiet place to cool off, she shouldn't see the angry Luca all the time"

Luca nodded," I'll keep that in mind"

"Great! Now, for our plan A, don't touch her for now" Harry announced.

Luca eyes dilated."Wh.....what?"

"Yes, let's just see if she wants you desperately too, give her space, keep your hands to yourself"

"You've got to be fucking kidding me, this is someone who makes me lose control of myself when I see her. Even if she wants me, she won't say it, she's shy and I'm gonna end up dying slowly"

"You have to do this, just for a while until you can figure out what she's feeling towards you now"

"This space shit is killing me" Luca muttered.

"You haven't even started the space shit!" Harry reminded, frustratedly.

"Is that all I need to do?"

"No, you have to give her gifts, don't give her anything that's too expensive, she might think you see her as a gold digger"

Luca rubbed his hand on his temple." You know, she reads too many books, her type always want romantic men. How can I….I mean… how do I behave so she'll think I'm romantic"

Harry fought the urge to laugh. Luca had always claimed to be perfect, now, he wanted to know how to be romantic.

"When it comes to women, they find most things you do romantic, like you have to say sweet words to her, she might pretend she doesn't like it but just one look at her cheeks would tell you otherwise."

Luca grinned, he had been making her smile and blush alot. He was making progress.

"Just act base on how you feel Luca. Now, please don't go against anything I said, we need to make this work, is that clear?"

Luca rolled his eyes," Crystal"

Maria walked out of the kitchen, she bumped into Luca and the bouquet he was holding fell from his hand.

"Shit!" He exclaimed and quickly picked it up, some flowers almost pulled off.

"Do you know how long I spent choosing this?" He asked, angrily.

Maria frowned." It's just flowers, Luca" She reminded.

"It isn't just flowers" He snapped.

She stared at him, confused.

"Where's Aryann?"

"Are those for Aryann?" Maria asked, amused.

"Hmmm, is anything wrong with me giving her flowers."

Maria shrugged.' Nothing, except the fact that you're acting weird' She thought.

"Now where's she?"

"She's watering the garden"

Luca teeth clenched." what about to the gardener?"

"She wanted to do it"

Luca took a deep breath, he didn't want her doing anything but he wouldn't let her know that. He glanced at Maria and walked away.

Luca walked into his garden, he saw her watering the plants in the garden, she seem to love what she was doing and he was glad.

"Hmmm" He cleared his throat announcing his presence.

She turned around to see him." Hey" She smiled.

He walked closer to her and stretched out the bouquet to her.

"I passed by a flower shop on my way home and saw how beautiful these looked, they reminded me of you" He said, softly.

She took the flowers from him." They are beautiful"

"You're beautiful" He replied, affectionately.

She smiled, broadly.

Luca stared at her white cotton t-shirt and flowery skirt, she wore a pair of flip flops on her slender feet. She had let her hair down, she definitely didn't need makeup to enhance her beauty.

"I'll just finish up here" she said and gently placed the bouquet on the rocking chair. she took the hose, trying to filled up the watering can again.

"I'll help you with that" Luca offered taking the watering can from the ground.

Aryann slowly started to filled up the watering can in his hand.

Water spilled on his chest.

"What the hell!" He exclaimed letting go of the watering can.

Aryann gasped." It wasn't intentional"

Luca smirked." Really?"

She didn't like the mischievous look he was giving her.

He reached out for another pipe.

"Luca" She warned.

But water splashed on her face.

"It wasn't intentional" He said mimicking her voice.

She grimaced slightly and turned on the hose to it's highest capacity and directed it towards him soaking his body completely.

"ARYANN!" He screamed.

She laughed." You started this" She accused.

"Fine! Bring it on "

And that was how they found themselves splashing water on each other, running, trying to duck each other's attack and laughing. At that, moment, Aryann saw him as an ordinary man, a man who wasn't out of her league.

Minutes later found them sitting on the rocking chair, exhausted.

"You don't know when to give up, do you?" Luca asked, staring at his drenched body.

"I don't and I won" She giggled.

Luca chuckled, she wasn't as wet as he was and that was because he had chosed to go easy on her, he didn't want her to fall sick.

Luca stared at her, aching to touch her, just hold her hand and maybe kiss her.

His eyes darted to her lips, just one kiss……one slight kiss.

"Keep your hands to yourself" Harry's words reeled through his mind.

And it took all the strength in him not to kiss her.

He quickly stood up.

"You must be cold, let's go in" He suggested and hurriedly started walking away.

Aryann stared at his wet body, lustfully. Why didn't he kiss her? Should she have made the first move?

Luca slowly turned on the shower trying to cool down his hard-on, this was pure torture and he wasn't sure how long he could keep up with this.

Next morning, Maria stared at Luca then at Aryann, they were all eating breakfast, and she had noticed that they were staring at each other when the other wasn't looking.

And she was at the middle of the strong eye connection. What was going on between them?

"I can't continue with this space shit any longer" Luca announced, he was with Harry in his company's eatery.

Harry stared at him in disbelief." It's has only been one night"

"That's so easy for you to say, if you have a plan B, let's go straight to it." He suggested, impatiently.

Harry smirked." Plan B"

"Take her out on a date" Harry suggested.

"A date? How's that gonna make her like me?"

"Women love dates."

"So where do I take her to?"

Harry sighed." I don't have to tell you everything, Luca, take her to a nice place, and before I forget, when you ask her out, don't make her feel she has to go whether she likes it or not, she should agree willingly"

"What if she says no?"

"I know you hate getting turned down but you have to accept it then I'll think of something else we could do"

Luca rubbed his hand on his temple. "Let's assume she says yes, how do I behave on the date?"

"Treat her like a queen, you can use this opportunity to tell her things she doesn't know about you but don't make her feel bored, then give her a gift, just something that she'll see every time and think of you"

"Alright then"

Luca thought about the previous day when they had played with water, just being with her makes him happy.

He smiled.

"And may I ask what you're thinking about?" Harry asked, curiously.

"It's just…. I didn't know it was possible to be this happy" He confessed.

Harry grinned." And I'm glad to see you smiling all the time, I'll be more than glad if this work out and you and Aryann would be in a proper relationship."

Luca nodded." Me too.

Aryann slowly hung her clothes into the closet. She turned around and her eyes caught the flowers he had given to her.

She knew she was falling hard and fast but she kept telling herself that she wasn't. Why did he keep on making her happy? She hadn't been this happy before and she was scared because this happiness was just temporary. Did he treat his past women like this? This was precisely what Ava had warned her about. Ava was more beautiful and sexy than her but Luca still got tired of her.

Aryann slowly sat on the bed, she wanted to feel nothing for him, she didn't want to think about him, she didn't want to care about him at all but she didn't know how to stop herself from doing that.

A knock sounded on the door, she stood up and walked towards it then opened it to find the only person who manage to easily turn her world upside down with just a touch…..a kiss…..a light caress.

"Hey" He began.

She forced a smile out of her.

Luca's eyes darted to her breasts, fuck! he wanted to see those ruby nipples or hers badly.

He had to pull himself together, she should want him desperately too but how much longer could he wait. His stared at her face, she looked sad.

He brought a hand to cup her jaw, the skin so silky-smooth and soft that he had to repress a groan of need." Are you okay"

Was he concerned about her? Her heart fluttered." I'm fine" She smiled, gladly ignoring her subconscious mind warning her that it was just a question.

"Do you have anything doing tomorrow? Like, do you have anywhere to go with Maria? He asked taking his hand away.

"No, why?"

Luca took a deep breath." I was wondering if you would like to.....you know.....go out with me, like...em...a date?" He drawled.

Aryann swallowed, a date with Luca? she didn't know how it would be like but she loved the sound of it.

"I'll love to go on a date with you, Luca" She agreed.

Luca smiled, relieved." Is 7:pm okay with you?"

"Yes" she replied waiting impatiently for him to pull her into his arms and kiss her.

"Okay then, goodnight" With that, he walked away.

Aryann sighed disappointedly. Luca was unpredictable.

She walked into her bedroom and shut the door then leaned against it.

This happiness wasn't going to last long but she would let herself feel it while it lasted.

"I hate jeans!" Luca complained for the umpteenth time. They were at the dressing room of a boutique. Harry had suggested he wore Jeans but he didn't have any in his closet.

He turned around to see Harry sitting on a chair and staring back at him.

"Won't you say anything?"

"I'm tired of convincing you that you look good in jeans" Harry snapped.

Luca stared at his reflection in the dressing mirror again. He was wearing a blue check shirt and black jeans.

"I really don't like this outfit, it doesn't make me feel...you know... powerful"

"Luca, you don't need to feel powerful tonight, you need to make her feel she's with a man who isn't off her league. Now I think those white sneakers would look great on you"

"I'm not wearing any sneakers" Luca retorted.

"You're so difficult, fine, at least wear the black, an Oxford shoe wouldn't look good on you today"

Luca grimaced slightly and agreed.

"If she's gonna like this, then it's worth it."

"I can't believe you're going on your first date at 32"Harry teased and laughed.

Luca shot him a glare.

"I told you to stop glaring at people" Harry reprimanded.

"I can't help it when it comes to you, you're the only moron in my life."

Harry scoffed." Really now? And what do you call someone who's taking advice from a moron?"

"You should feel honored that I'm listening to you"

Harry gasped." Some things really can't change about you, don't ruin this date, Luca"He warned.

Luca smirked." Don't worry, nothing would go wrong"

Maria stared at Aryann's bed, startled by the clothes everywhere.

"I can't find anything to wear" She complained.

"Where are you going?"Maria asked walking closer to her.

"Luca's taking me out on a date this evening" She announced, excitedly.

Maria frowned. Luca? Date?

"How does his past women dress on their dates? Aryann asked, curiously.

"He has never taken any woman out on a date before"

Aryann felt butterflies letting loose in her stomach. She was the first?

"Luca likes this kind of dresses" Maria said showing her a short sleeveless red dress which would obviously make half of her breasts to be exposed.

"He doesn't" Aryann replied, calmly.

"How do you know that? Didn't he like the black dress you wore to the company's party?"

Aryann knew he didn't seem to like that dress, she couldn't really say the reason though but he had said he saw alot of men staring lustfully at her and that was something he didn't like.

"He didn't like it, I just want something simple" She replied and her eyes caught a purple dress, she picked it up, it was short sleeves and flared.

She smiled." I think I'll go with this"

Maria stared at the dress." It's beautiful."

She agreed and stared at the smile on Aryann's face, she knew Aryann was getting shaken emotionally by Luca and Luca….well, she didn't want to jump into any conclusions but she was scared for Aryann.

She had seen alot of women cry while leaving this house and she didn't want Aryann to be on that list.

Luca leaned against the door of his car, he wasn't going out with any of his men tonight, it would just be him and Aryann.

He heard a sound from the front door of his house, he lifted up his head. He forgot to breathe. Aryann was………..He didn't even know which word to use to describe her look. She'd let down her hair and they were flowing on her shoulders, her face devoid of makeup. His gaze traveled downwards, to her neckline then breasts, he smiled relieved that it was well covered with the gown, he would go nuts if he had to put up with men staring at them again.

His gaze skimmed Aryann's flat stomach and lingered on the gentle flare of her hips. Her feet were encased in white heels. His head felt curiously light, his crotch most unsurprisingly heavy.

This woman was mercilessly tempting him.

"You look nice…no not just nice and…em… pretty and….."

"Thank you" She cut in, softly.

Chapter seven

Aryann stared at what he was wearing, his hair was gelled backwards, his blue shirt clung to his wide shoulders and powerful chest and the jeans accentuated the long muscular strength of his legs and the lean tautness of his hips.

He looked more masculine and sexy than he normally did.

Her mouth ran dry, the colour in her cheeks heightening as she briefly relived the intensity of having his hot mouth in hers.

"You don't look bad either" She choked out.

Luca sent a self-conscious glance at his jeans." Do you like jeans? I don't remember when last I wore Jeans, don't I look……."

"You look good, Luca. And you also look good in suits" She confessed.

Luca's heart leapt, he smiled boyishly, it was his turn to blush, she always admired him in suits?

Aryann stared at the smile on his handsome face, if he wasn't gonna kiss her soon then she'll have to take those lips in hers.

Luca realized he was wasting time.

He quickly opened the door for her.

"Thank you" She smiled and got into the car, he closed the door gently.

Luca hurried around the car and got in.

He moved closer to her and for a breathtaking moment, she thought he was going to kiss her but then he drew out the seatbelt.

"Fasten your seatbelt" He whispered and moved away from her.

She gulped and slowly fastened her seatbelt.

"Where are we going" She asked curiously.

Luca slung her a grin." Wait for it, ma Belle!

Knowing what that meant, instantly, everything seemed lighter and brighter.

Almost thirty minutes later.

Luca got down from his car and quickly went over to open her door.

She smiled and got down too, and stared at the restaurant in front of her.

"Te amo?"She gasped.

Luca frozed" Have you been here before?"

"No, it's just... I've heard so many things about this place" She replied.

Luca grimaced." And did you like what you heard?"

Aryann nodded.

He slowly took her hand making their fingers entwined." Then I can assure you that you'll like it here" He assured and they headed towards the restaurant.

Aryann stared at their hands, she felt uneasy with Luca holding her like this but if he lets go, she knew she would be disappointed.

"Te amo"

As she stepped into the restaurant, she stared around in awe, she couldn't believe she was here with Luca. She had read online that the restaurant was owned by an Argentinian, and he had simply named it in his language, the name expresses love. And then, the dance floor was always opened for couples to tango.

Will Luca ask her to dance with him? She had forgotten some steps in tango. Does he even know how to tango?

They slowly sat down. Luca smiled proudly on seeing the delight in her eyes as she looked around the restaurant.

He slowly handed her the menu.

"Mr Herron" Someone called, They both looked up to see a man probably in his early forties standing beside their table.

"I'm Rico Romero, the manager, I'm so honored having someone like you here today" He said, gladly extending his hand for a handshake.

Luca shook his hand.

He turned to face Aryann." It's nice having you here ma'm"

Aryann grinned uneasily.

"When it's time to dance, I want a very strong beat" Luca requested.

"Anything you say, sir"Rico replied and walked away.

"My presence is quite fabulous, isn't it?" He asked, proudly.

Aryann rolled her eyes, he was still a proud peacock.

"I can see that" She replied, sarcastically.

Luca placed his hand over his mouth, he had to work on his perfect issues.

"Have you decided on what you'll like to eat?" He asked.

"Chicken pilaf" She replied.

Luca nodded and ran the bell, a waiter sauntered in.

"We'll like to have chicken pilaf and beef steak" He ordered.

"A bottle of red wine will do too" He added.

The waiter nodded and walked away.

"Can you tango? She asked curiously.

"Yeah"

"Seriously?" she asked in disbelief.

Luca frowned." What do you take me for? Woman, I'm good at everything" He said, proudly.

"Where did you learn how to tango?" She asked.

She could see his face drained of colour. Was that a bad question?

At that moment, the waiter walked in serving them what he had ordered for.

He picked up his Knife and slice into his steak.

"Let's eat" He suggested, faintly.

She picked up her spoon and without a word or glance at him, she started eating.

They ate in silence. When they were satisfied, the waiter cleared the table leaving the wine and two glasses, Luca filled the two glasses with wine and placed a glass in front of her.

"My mother taught me how to tango, she was from Buenos Aires, the times she gave me her attention was mainly spent dancing tango"

He wasn't looking at her, he was looking at his glass of wine, staring at the ruby-red depth.

Aryann winced inwardly." You don't have to tell me if…….."

He met her gaze." I want to tell you" He cut in, calmly.

His mouth thinned." My dad didn't like to dance with her, he said tango steps were too difficult. So she made me dance with her instead, at first, I hated tango, it made me always exhausted but she would never let me be, so I started hiding each time she was ready to dance, I would hide in my closet, and when she catches me, we would start playing 'catch me if you can" Luca laughed.

Aryann grinned imagining a little boy hiding and running away from his mother simply because he didn't want to dance with her.

Luca continued" Eventually, she would promise to buy me ice cream and then I will have no other choice but to dance with her. She took me to Argentina one summer holiday, and while there we visited a milonga, when I saw how couples danced tango so well, it was the most beautiful thing I have ever seen, people lost in a world of their own, I loved tango from that day and my mom didn't have to run after me to dance with her again."

Aryann smiled, she was happy that he didn't only have bad memories of his parents, and she was more than happy that he had told her about this.

"But that was years ago, can you still dance tango very well? Have you been dancing with someone?"

"No, I didn't dance tango after my mom passed, but I have following up new milonguero styles online and yes, I can still tango very well" He said, proudly.

And then, some couples started hurrying off to the dance floor.

Luca stood up and stretched forth one hand to her.

"May I have this dance?"

"I don't think I know all the styles" She muttered.

"Don't worry, you just have to follow my lead" He smiled.

She took his hand and he led her to the dance floor.

They stood before each other, she lifted her chin helplessly, eyes snarled by his. He reached out and hooked a hand to the back of her neck drawing her closer to him, slowly and inexorably. He took her right hand and lifted it up to his shoulder. His other hand moved slowly down to her waist.

His arm across her back then Aryann closed her eyes in a moment of confusion, his touch was having an explosive effect on her.

She moved so that she leaned into him fully and expertly Luca started to dance, twisting and turning Aryann in a series of moves.

Her natural dance ability and instinct took over as she recognized his lead and followed him.

She unconsciously let him take more of her weight. Their steps became more complex.

Her head turned in the same direction as his, tucked perfectly just below his jaw.

They fitted perfectly!

His movements were graceful. His steps following the beats in a rhythmic order of…..slow…. slow……. quick….. quick…….slow.

Aryann felt like she was in another world, a world where she could stay like this dancing with Luca forever. This man…… with his arms wrapped strongly around her…….was something she never wished to go out from.

Her head fell back and he bent too, holding her possessively as the music ended.

Their eyes locked, breath falling and rising like a tandem.

They were brought back to reality by the sounds of applauds around them, he stood up straight, taking her hand in his.

People had stopped dancing a while ago to watch them.

Luca smiled proudly. Were they that good?

He waved at the different elegant couples then he made his way out of the restaurant with his lady.

"And where did you learn how to dance tango like that?" Luca asked, curiously.

"Cole taught me" She blurted out.

He stopped dead in his track taking his hand away from hers as hurt flashed through his eyes.

"Cole?" He choked out.

Cole taught her how to dance so beautifully? How many times did they dance together? Did she still feel something for him? He would have been more relaxed if they hadn't seen each other at the party.

He suddenly felt angry. He was trying his best to make her like him when she probably liked someone else.

"Don't ruin this date, Luca"

Harry's words ran through his head.

"Let's get going" He said, coldly and started to walk away.

Aryann stared at him surprised by his cold behaviour, she knew he didn't like Cole, he had said he didn't want her thinking about another man while he still wanted her. Was he having that thought? She wasn't thinking about Cole, and definitely not romantically too. She didn't want anything to ruin this beautiful date.

She quickly hurried towards him.

She held his arm.

"I had danced tango before and I thought it was fun, but with you, it's different" She confessed.

Abruptly, he turned around. She felt the heat too.

Aryann heaved a sigh of relief on seeing his eyes softened.

"Are you still in touch with him.....Cole I mean?"

"No"

He rubbed his hand down his face in a slow yet frenzied motion. He didn't want to know if she still liked him or the things Cole might have done for her. He might not be able to handle it, this jealousy of his was extremely bad.

"I know I'm not fun to be with, but em....did you like the date?" He asked, nervously.

Aryann smiled." I loved it and I will like to dance tango with you again, you are certainly the best milonguero I've seen"

A slow smile curved Luca's sensual mouth and, aghast at the liquid pooling of heat in her belly, she raised up on her toes and pressed her mouth to his.

She felt his body stiffen and then she realized that they were in public. She tried to pull away but he wouldn't let her.

He bent his head, then paused before his mouth touched hers. She sucked in her breath.

"Luca…."She bit out as her eyes closed.

Slowly, he drew her into his arms. The first kiss was gentle.

He pulled back then dipped his head again and nibbled gently on her lower lip.

"You taste good" He whispered, trying to slow his own fervor. It was difficult.

Her gaze met his, he could see desire in those incredible whiskey-coloured eyes of hers.

He captured her mouth in another kiss. When she didn't resist, he ran his tongue over the seam of her lips. With a soft whimper, she opened for him and allowed him inside to taste her again. When Luca heard people's voices and laughter, he broke off the kiss and pressed his forehead against hers.

"I think this place is getting too crowded. I want to be alone with you in the worst way"

He felt her trembling in his arms." I want that too" She admitted.

Luca took her hand and they headed for the parking lot.

"Can I drive?" She asked, politely.

"You know how to drive?" He asked.

She nodded.

Luca suppressed his lips in a tight line, he didn't want to ask who taught her cause it might just be Cole again.

And he was damn right. It was indeed Cole.

He gave her the car mobiliser as soon as they got to the parking lot.

They slid into the car and she started it.

Slowly, she rode away.

Luca stared at her hands on the steering wheel, she was incredibly slow but he liked it, at least, it would give him more time to stare at her.

"You're distracting me" She muttered.

Luca frowned." I didn't say anything"

"You keep staring at me"

Luca chuckled." I can't help it, not when you're so pretty"

Heat drenched her cheeks. "Luca, I can't focus" She groaned.

"Sorry ma'm" He said, sarcastically.

"Did you know your birth father?" He asked changing the topic to a more safer realm.

"I didn't, I don't even know how he looks like and he probably doesn't know I exist, but I heard my mom saying on few occasions that he was called Phillip. Whenever I asked about him, she always didn't want to talk about him and she didn't have any pictures of him, I guess she was deeply felt hurt by his rejection"

Luca grimaced slightly." Was Edward nice to you?"

"He wasn't, but he didn't hit me, my mom did though when I was little. Then I'd watch how Edward played with Nicole and I would wish he could call me to play too, but he never did. I don't hate him though, at least, he gave me a roof over my head and sponsored me through elementary and high school"

"You didn't go to college?"

"I went to a three year program in college but I studied part time, I had to work to pay my fees"

Luca sighed. Edward was really something. He was glad he had given Aryann to him and not his daughter. No one could be like Aryann. All he needed now was to prove to her that he could change, he could be a better person.

"Didn't you have any friends?" He asked, curiously.

"I did, but we weren't really close, did you have any friends apart from Harry?"

Luca sighed." I didn't. People were quite scared of being close to me, I sometimes wonder why Harry wasn't. I was mean to him after my parents died. He would always want me to go to the park with him and his parents and I felt he pitied me, so I would say mean things to him so he would stop coming to see me, when he wouldn't stop coming, I broke his favorite toy. He didn't speak to me for days. And when it was my birthday, he sent me a gift, I can never forget what he wrote."

"What did he write to you?"

"Hey jerk! You are bad and that's good, you can't be good and that's not bad, and I don't want you to be anything else but you, you're not just my best friend, you're my brother"

Aryann grinned." And what did you do after that?"

Luca cocked an eyebrow." someone loves my gist" He teased.

She glanced at him.

Luca shrugged." Well, I went to a toy store and bought the exact toy I broke, I gave it to him and we made up but I wouldn't say we didn't quarrel after that but somehow, we still made up"

She knew Luca would be the cause of all their fights but she loved the bond between them.

"Red light!" Luca thundered snapping her out from her thoughts, she quickly stepped on the brakes and heaved a sigh of relief, she had almost ran into a car in front of her.

She couldn't bring herself to look at him, he must be furious.

"You're such a terrible driver!" He teased.

Aryann slowly stared at him.

"You distracted me" She accused.

Luca chuckled," it not my fault that you love stories."

Aryann laughed.

Aryann slowly came to a halt in the parking lot of Luca's house.

"I had a good time today" He said, suddenly feeling as nervous as an adolescent boy.

"Me too" She replied wishing she could spend every day like this with Luca.

He brought out something from his pocket. He held her hand and she felt something clamped around her wrist.

He took his hand away and she gazed at a gold bracelet. At the middle was a bold inscription.

'MINE'

"I want you to….to remember this day, we could go on other dates but this one is so special to me, and by our next date, I'll be a better milonguero for you" He assured, innocuously.

Aryann smiled, she ran a finger through the bracelet, it gave her some kind of assurance that he might no longer see her as his plaything.

She brought out her cellphone.

"Let's take a selfie" She suggested.

"I hate taking pictures" He snapped.

"Please Luca" She pleaded and he couldn't say no to her.

He moved closer to her and she took one selfie.

She turned to face him." You didn't even smile"

"I don't like to smile, it makes me feel weak"

Aryann scoffed." But I have seen you smile alot recently" She reminded.

"That's because I'm with you"

Her heart fluttered." Now, please, will you smile for me?" She asked, sweetly.

Luca grinned.' You're making me blush' He thought and moved closer to her again, he smiled as she took the selfie.

"I have a few pictures of you" He confessed.

She frowned," Really?"

"Yes" He brought out his cellphone from his pocket, he unlocked it and slid into the gallery. He gave the phone to her.

Aryann gasped, they were pictures of her sleeping, one, her lips were parted probably snoring. The other one, her left hand was on her head, she looked stupid.

As she pressed delete, he grabbed his phone from her.

"What the hell do you think you're doing?"

"Please delete it, I look crazy." She pleaded.

Luca stared at the pictures, recalling the sense of joy it always gives him to watch her sleep.

"They're beautiful"

Aryann sighed, there was no way she could win against him.

"Fine, but please take me new ones now that I'm awake, I can assure you they would look more beautiful"

"Awake or asleep, you're beautiful" He assured.

She smiled." Even so, Please take me new ones" She pressed on.

Luca shrugged.

She quickly gave her best smile as he took her some shots.

Luca stared at her picture on his phone. Fuck space!

He reached for her and before she could react, everything disappeared as his mouth crashed down on hers.

The entire world seemed to explode inside her head, his mouth was hard and hot.

He slowly took his mouth away, staring into her eyes, she had to suck in a breath at the intensity of his dark eyes, and could see his gaze moved to her throat, where she could feel the beat of her traitorous pulse underneath her skin.

"Aryann, I want you to know how much I want you but I'd never force you into anything again" He started to move away.

She took hold of his shirt to stop him.

"I want to be with you tonight, too."

That was all he needed to hear. He dipped his head and kissed her again.

Aryann held herself still, fighting the sharp sensation of wanting…. needing…….that Luca awakened in her so easily. A tightening of belly muscles, a heaviness in her breasts, a yearning in her heart. For a heartbeat, the parking lot melted away, she saw only Luca.

His mouth parted hers, his tongue tracing her lower lip until she opened fully. He swept inside and she drank him with a sigh. Before she quite knew what had happened, she was in his laps, arms around his neck. God! how she loved touching him, loved kissing him. If she could crawl into his skin, she would've done it.

He gripped her hips….hard and rocked her against his erection. Hot pleasure spiraled through Aryann's body.

He impatiently lifted her up a bit then he tugged down his jeans and boxers.

He reached into her dress, he held her panties, on second thought, he ripped them off her. "Sorry, this have to go" He said impatiently dropping them on the floor but she didn't seem to care.

His cock was hard, lifting her hips, he eased her down on his erection. She grabbed the headrest as she regained her seated position…..but this time with him inside her body.

He wrapped his arms around her. She moaned. He held himself still savoring the feeling of being within her. It felt even better. He kissed her neck. When he could stand his inaction no longer, he rocked, surging inside her. He smiled against her neck as a sexy moan dragged from her throat.

She gasped as he stroked upward inside her. She started moving up and down his cock, but when he moved and stroked her deeply, she covered her mouth with her hand.

He quickly took her hand away.

"I want you to scream, no one can hear you so scream my name, baby!" He screamed.

"Lu……ca" she gasped as he moved hotly into her.

He held her hips and grind her more deeply against his cock, and in no time she was screaming in esctasy.

He didn't know how long they stayed in the car but even after reliving the hot, tight, wet seal of her body round his, he still wanted more.

Almost an hour later found them sitting on the bed in her room watching a movie. Luca had been delighted when she had wanted to watch a movie with him.

But now, he still found it strange as to what people found in movies. It was boring. He decided to focus his attention on her, she was always fascinating to look at. He stared at her eyes, they were focused greatly on the TV, then to her perfect nose and her lips, he smiled. She keeps getting beautiful.

He slowly looked away from her, how would she react to his confession, he wasn't expecting her to feel the same already but he wanted her to at least give him a chance.

He was snapped out of his thoughts when he heard soft sobs coming from her direction. Instantly, he turned to face her, holding her jaw quite alarmed.

"Why are you crying?" He asked, tensed.

"She……she died" Aryann choked out.

Luca frowned and turned to look at the TV, he realized that the female lead died in the movie.

"I can't believe you're crying because of that" He snapped. He was slightly relieved that this had nothing to do with him, but he didn't feel good at all seeing her tears.

He grabbed the remote and turned off the TV.

"How could you turned it off, someone just died!" She yelled trying to stem her tears.

Luca sighed." someone died in the movie Aryann, and I can't stand those tears of yours" He retorted and stood up from the bed to look for a handkerchief so she could wipe her face thoroughly. He headed for her closet.

She quickly jumped out of the bed and stood in front of the closet.

"You can't open this" She said

Luca frowned." why?"

"Because …..em…. I"

"Are you hiding something from me" He asked, suspiciously.

"No"

Luca gently pulled her out of his way and opened the closet, he saw her old clothes neatly arranged beside the ones he had bought for her.

He grinned and turned to face her, she quickly got on the bed and covered her whole body with the duvet.

He walked up to the bed and pulled it off her body.

"You are one stubborn and sexy lady" He teased.

She smiled knowing that he wasn't upset .

"How should I punish you?"

Her smile faded.

"Should I fuck you till Maria comes to ask 'what is going on?" He asked, smiling mischievously.

He could see the colour in her cheeks heightening.

"You love the sound of that, don't you?" He asked crawling into the bed.

"No" She lied.

"Don't worry, Maria knows when to stay away from this" He assured.

"Now, do you want that?" He asked again.

"I want you" she bit out.

He cupped her face with one hand, his eyes grew dark and intensed as he studied her.

A smile warmed her insides as he kissed her. The kiss turned hot, desperate, needy and made her heart pound with excitement.

She raked her hands down his chest and reached for his shirt, then peeled it off him. When her warm fingers caressed his chest, he nearly came apart. He groaned and placed his hand over hers.

"Aryann, you do unbelievable things to me"

"Really?" She sounded surprised.

"Really" He repeated and planted kisses along her throat and neck, nibbled at her ear, spiking her own fever.

She bent and kissed his chest, her fingers dancing across it in a sensuous parade that made his breath hitched.

He slowly took off her clothes and kissed her neck again as one hand cupped her breasts. Her nipples budded beneath his touch, aching for more.

Seconds later, their touch turned frantic, passionate.

Hunger for him triggered a desperation that she'd never felt before. And when he closed his lips over one pebbled nipple, she closed her eyes, sensation spiraling through her body teemed with pleasure.

He trailed his tongue across Aryann's breasts. He wanted her so badly, his sex throbbed to be inside her, his heart racing with the urgency to have her.

She clung to him, her hunger palpable in the soft moans she elicited, her hands urging him closer as he rose above her. Needing to taste her, he planted kisses down her breasts to her stomach, then slid his fingers to her heat.

She arched against him and stroked his calf with her foot, then wrapped one leg around him, urging him between her thighs.

His body hardened and he rocked himself against her teasing her femininity with his erection. Her breathing grew ragged, hurried with excitement, he moved down her body and parted her thighs with his hands.

He closed his lips over her heat.

Aryann dug her fingers into his hair and murmured a soft "yes" her body quivering as he teased and tormented her with his tongue. And when he lifted her hips to taste her sweetness, she cried out his name and came with a fierceness that almost sent him over the edge.

He let her ride the wave of pleasure, his own spiked by the sound of her whispering his name. He took off his remaining clothes then rose above her, knead her legs about and nudged her with his hard length.

Aryann slipped her hand down to stroke him, and mindless sensation ripped through him. He stroked her over and over, his blood was on fire as she guided him inside her. The moment he felt her body clench around his, his own release was imminent. But he prolonged the pleasure as long as he could, easing out of her and thrusting inside her warmth again and again. Finally, he angled her hips so he could drive himself deeper until he filled her and she cried out again with another orgasm.

He came then, swiftly, intensely and he gripped her hips and closed his eyes, emotions pummeling him as she completed him.

Aryann's body quivered with sensations as she curled into Luca's arms.

Making love with him had been intense, mind-numbing and so erotic that she never wanted it to end. He wrapped his arms around her and stroked her hair, his strong arms, a fortress that would protect her from the world.

"Sex with you sizzles everytime" He told her, appreciatively.

It was a perfect time to tell her that he loves her but he quickly discarded that thought, it had been a long night, morning now, and he wanted her to get some sleep.

The following evening, Aryann was bubbling with joy, she wanted to watch a movie with Luca again and hurriedly made her way to his study. As she held the doorknob, what she heard made her feel like a thousand bullet shattering through her chest.

"She means nothing to me, Harry."

"C'mon, you know what I do with my past playthings, it's just sex!"

Aryann stumbled blindly back to the hall and headed like a homing pigeon for the stairs again to take cover in the privacy of her room.

FEW MINUTES EARLIER........

Luca sat on the swivel chair in his study. He wasn't able to concentrate with work today, he needed to tell her soon, he didn't know how to make it romantic, Harry wasn't at work today so he had no one to talk to.

He picked up his cellphone and dialed Harry's number.

"Hey bro" Harry began.

Luca could hear shuffling in the background.

"What are you doing?"

"Cooking, so why did you call?"

"I wanna tell Aryann how I feel about her"

"She's in your house" Harry reminded.

"No, I don't just wanna walk up to her and tell her, I want it to be special and romantic,
even if she doesn't feel the same, she might give me a chance"

"So…..oh, that reminds me, you won't believe who I saw today"

Luca frowned." Who?"

"Ava"

"And what's so special about her?"

"She's dating Lewis, I think she's doing that to spite you"

Luca sighed, Lewis was his biggest rival.

"She means nothing to me, Harry"

"Really? Ava was breathtakingly gorgeous, you mean you didn't even feel a thing for her,
what then….."

"C'mon, you know what I do with my past playthings, it's just sex!"

Chapter eight

PRESENTLY………

"What about Aryann?"

Luca's heart leapt at the mention of her name.

"Aryann isn't my plaything, she's my lady, she's the sunshine that lights up my heart, she brightens my day with just her smile, if I keep saying what she does to me, we would be on the phone for hours"

He could hear Harry giggled." I'm so glad that you found someone who makes you happy and to hear you talk about her like that is priceless."

"Now, will you please help me"

"Woah! this is serious, Luca just begged me to help him" He mocked.

"Ha ha" Luca said, sarcastically.

"Hmm…. let's see, I can picture a romantic dinner, let's just say a candle lit dinner, at your garden, you'll have to make sure she doesn't go there though, it has to be a surprise. Then you guys can eat and talk and most importantly, dance tango, since you said it's passionate with her, after that, tell her how you feel, tell her everything"

Luca sighed." A candle lit dinner? I can't set it up"

"Relax, that's why you've got me, I'll be there tomorrow by noon, we don't need any event planner, she'll be swept off her feet to know that we did it ourselves"

Luca smiled." Thanks Harry"

"You're welcome, sir Luca, now, get your acts together, nothing should ruin this" Harry warned.

"Got it"

"She means nothing to me, Harry"

Luca's words ran through her head.

She tried to shake it off but the pain in her chest won't go away.

She quickly sat on her bed and brought out her e-reader. She needed to forget about everything.

She tapped on a novel titled "Dream guy" and started reading.

She couldn't comprehend anything.

"She means nothing to me, Harry"

Those were the only words flowing through her head. She placed the e-reader on the bed and stared at her bracelet.

Nothing? It's just sex? then why has he been acting so sweet to her? Why did he take her out on a date? Just why?

This was what Ava had warned her about. He had made him fall headlong in love with him but was never going to reciprocate those feelings.

The thought of that sent tears rolling down her cheeks, she angrily brushed them away with the back of her hand but they won't stop coming, thick and fast.

She sat on the floor and wept, trying to tell herself that she was crying because of the grief of the past.

But who was kidding? She was crying for the fact that she had never loved anyone this much before, that she wanted to be loved too.

She wanted to mean something to him, but that was like asking for wings to fly. As tears kept on soaking her shirt, she knew she couldn't do this anymore, she couldn't continue being his sex-toy and keep getting emotionally wrung out, she would just wither and die.

Luca walked into her bedroom, he found her lying on the bed, she was already asleep.

He grinned and moved closer to the bed, he grabbed the duvet and covered her body.

His heart clenched painfully taking in the look on her face.

Dried tear mark left silver lining trailing down her cheeks.

She cried? And it seemed she cried alot too, he stared at the TV, she didn't seem to have watched a movie and a tragedy won't make her cry this much.

He stared at the e-reader beside her and picked it up. He turned it on and realized that she was reading a novel, titled "Dream guy".

The first three lines gave him all the answers to his questions.

"The man of my dreams is not him. He has ruined everything, he has ruined me and at the end, I can never be happy"

He couldn't read more, he gently placed the e-reader on the table.

This had definitely made her cry! It had reminded her of what she wanted. Her dream guy.

He could never be the man of her dreams, who probably didn't have anger issues, who was romantic, who would never make her cry.

He thought they had gone passed that stage, when she'd always cry herself to sleep because of him. But she still cried and the thought that it might be frequent tore him apart.

Luca slowly poured himself a measure of whiskey with a shaky hand………a shaky hand.

He brought the glass close to his lips and winced slightly as it burnt it way down his throat.

He was in his kitchen, sitting on a stool in the breakfast bar.

She cried………

He couldn't stop thinking about those tear stained cheeks of hers.

Who was he to think that he made her happy simply because he could make her smile and laugh.

Who could ever be happy with a man who took her by force, who deflowered her against her wishes?

Who would be happy with a monster? He knew he shouldn't call himself that but he felt like one tonight.

He should have let her go when his feelings weren't this strong. Then again, was there anytime when his feelings weren't all consuming.

A sound came from the door, he slightly looked up and saw her walk in.

She opened the refrigerator and took a bottle of water. As she turned around, she stopped on seeing him.

Luca stared at the desolate look in her eyes, he couldn't do this anymore, he couldn't ignore her unhappiness and he couldn't put up with it, he couldn't change how she felt about him but he had to give her what she wanted.

"Do you…….do you want me to let you go?" He asked.

"Please say no" He thought.

"Yes" She replied, bluntly.

He felt shattered, he slowly stood up.

"It's late, I'll tell Raph to drop you off tomorrow" He said, gruffly and headed for the door.

He paused at the door.

"I'm sorry, I'm truly sorry for everything" And with that, he walked away.

Shockwaves rolled over Aryann.

Just like that? He didn't even try……he didn't even……..

Tears threatened but she fought them back, she wouldn't cry anymore.

She had to be strong, she had to be okay.

☐

Luca stared at his door, he had left it wide open, she might change her mind, she might want to still be with him.

She might give him a chance to prove to her that he could be a good person.

He stared at the wall clock as the hours ticked by then it was morning.

"Don't leave me, Aryann….. please" He muttered.

Maria stared at Aryann as Raph placed her things in the boot of the car.

This is what she had always wanted, she had always pleaded with Luca to let Aryann go, then why did she feel so devastated?

Aryann turned to face her.

She brought out the envelope filled with money that Luca had insisted she gives to her.

"Luca wanted you to have this" Maria said.

Aryann stared at the envelope, was she getting paid for being his whore?

"I don't want it" She replied.

Maria sighed." But what would you do, dear? You said you ain't going back to your Edward's house"

"I saw a small and portable apartment online yesterday, I called the owner and she said I could come check it out today. I have some money saved up, don't worry, Maria, I'll be fine" Aryann assured.

Maria sighed deeply and hugged her tightly.

"I'm gonna miss you so much"

"Me too" Aryann bit out, Maria had been like a mother to her.

After sometime, they disengaged from each other. Aryann looked behind her, she wanted to see him just one more time but he was nowhere.

She nodded positively, she'd get through this.

"Goodbye, Maria"

"Goodbye, Aryann" Maria replied with tears filled eyes.

Luca opened his curtains, he looked down and saw her slid into his car. Raph drove away.

She left……..

It was like a part of him has been violently cut off.

He slumped heavily on his bed in a sitting position.

Maria walked into his room.

"She didn't take the money" She began and placed the envelope on top his table.

"Is she going back to Edward's house?"

"No, she said she had some money saved up, she's gonna rent an apartment"

"Oh"

"I don't quite get you, you were treating her differently, with the date and all, I know I shouldn't have jump into conclusion like that but I thought you were falling in love with her"

"I love her" He said, ruefully.

"Then why did you let her go?" Maria asked, confused.

"She doesn't want to be here, she was unhappy" He sighed deeply and added" It was the best thing to do"

Maria heaved a sigh of comprehension, she was sure that Aryann wasn't aware of how Luca felt toward her, she knew Aryann felt something for him too. Why couldn't he speak up sooner?

"But………"

"It's better this way!" He yelled, lividly, startling hell out of Maria.

She simply nodded and walked away.

Harry walked into Luca's house excitedly.

He found Maria sitting on the couch in the living room, he scanned the place but didn't see Aryann.

"Where's Aryann?"

"She left" Maria announced.

Harry frozed." Left? as in?

"Luca told her that she could leave"

"What?"

Luca stared at the pictures of Aryann on his cellphone, he should have taken more.

"What the hell is wrong with you?" Harry asked walking into his room.

Luca sighed," I don't wanna talk about it"

"I came here so we could set up a candle light dinner. I can't understand this, we were making progress, why………."

"She fucking cried!" Luca yelled.

Harry frowned.

"When I didn't care, I could keep her here as long as I want but I want her to be happy, I would continue to break apart if I continue making her unhappy, she wanted to leave, she doesn't love me, I hurt her so many times, all……all this is my fault" Luca yelled.

"Don't be……."

"Don't even say anything to justify what I did….. I'm a bad person, I can't be good enough, I can never be her dream guy" He choked out.

She was gone…..He was never going to touch her again, he was never going to see her
smile again, she's going to forget about him and move on.
Tears flooded his eyes, he tried hard not to blink, he couldn't cry because of a woman.
But the tears dropped, followed by more, falling down in thick sheet.
His heart was aching so painfully and it was as if he was going to die from it.

Harry stared at him quite stunned. He knew Luca really loved Aryann but he didn't know
that it was this much.
"Leave, Harry" He choked out amidst tears.
Harry knew better not to argue with him any further, he knew Luca was already feeling
pathetic and he didn't want anyone to see him this way.
He slowly walked away. Harry raked his hand through his hair as he made his way
downstairs. He walked into the living room and sat down on a chaise lounge adjacent to
Maria.
"I don't like the way things are, Maria" He bit out.
"Me too" She agreed.
"You were the closest to Aryann, I know things didn't start off in the right way, but didn't
you noticed anything about her, didn't she like Luca at all?"
"Well, I know she cared about him, she was quite excited about the date and she obviously
missed him when he traveled to France"
Harry sighed, Luca should've told her how he felt sooner but it was too late now.

Aryann slowly cleaned up her apartment, she was happy it came furnished though the
couch was nothing to write home about but she liked it.
She was okay with everything, she could handle this turn of her life just fine.
The apartment was small, just a living room, a bedroom, bathroom, toilet and kitchen. The
rent was affordable. She had gone grocery shopping and still had a few cash left to spare.
As she rounded up her cleaning, she walked into her bedroom and brought out her
planner, she had to start looking for a job tomorrow, she had to be mindful of the way she
spent her remaining amount of money before she would receive her paycheck after getting
her job.
She slowly put away the planner, she was on her own now, she had nobody, it was just
her against the world.
"I can't keep my eyes off you, do you know how beautiful you are when you're asleep in
my arms?"

"Can't you be less pretty?"

"You're beautiful"

"You should smile all the time, I hate seeing your tears"

"Someone loves my gist"

Memories reeled through her mind, what was he doing right now? was he thinking about her? even just a little, did he feel this yearning too.

He probably didn't have the time for that, tears stung her eyes, but she wouldn't let it fall, she wouldn't cry because of him, it was useless doing so, it won't change anything, it would only make her feel miserable.

She stared at the bracelet on her wrist, wasn't it insane to want to forget someone but at the same time, you want a constant reminder of him?

She had taken the e-reader too. Even if they could never be together again, she was still glad that he was a part of her life.

She thought about how it always felt to have his mouth on hers, to have his mouth on her nipples…..on her skin….. between her legs.

Then his longer fingers which always made her begged for more and his cock……..oh!

Without realizing it, her hand travelled over to her breasts, absently twisting her nipple over her dress, closing her eyes, she let out a breath she didn't know she'd been holding as the touch of her own hands turned into those in her memory.

His long graceful fingers ghosting along her breasts, his thumb brushing her nipples as he cupped, squeezed and caressed her breasts. Damn! It always felt so good.

She lay flat on the bed, she had to stop thinking about him, she needed a distraction.

She quickly brought out her cellphone and scanned the internet for any job opportunities. She found two vacancies in KM finance and Mobilotech.

She smiled and quickly put her pen into action writing an application.

When she finally fell asleep, her dreams are clouded with an incredibly handsome man with dark golden eyes dancing tango with her.

Nearly two days later……

Aryann walked out of KM finance excitedly, she had just been employed, though that wasn't the position she had anticipated for, someone else got it and luckily for her, they were in need of a new receptionist.

The pay was more than okay and she was happy. She'd been to Mobilotech the previous day but there were no more vacancies.

Aryann nodded positively, she would be happy again, this was a good start in her life.

The following morning, she was dressed smartly in blue long sleeves and black skirt, her feet was encased in black loafers.
She stood in front of the dressing mirror and pulled her hair into a bun.
She sighed satisfied by her looks. She held the bracelet in her wrist, she wanted to take it off but she was scared to, she was scared to think that one day, she would be with another man, Luca would be with another woman, the both of them would move on.
She knew that was the best thing to do but she didn't want to forget about him. At least…not so soon.
She brought out her cellphone, unlocked it and slid into the gallery. She ran a finger through his face on the screen, if there was a next life, she wanted them to meet again, but in that life, Luca would love her too.
Tears threatened but refused to cry again.
She quickly shoved all the things she needed into her bag and hurried off to work.

Aryann walked out of her apartment building, her footsteps halted at who she saw approaching……….. Nicole and one of her numerous boyfriends.
"Look who we have here" Nicole sneered, standing in front of her.
"Hey" Aryann said, dryly.
"I saw you coming out from that building, Luca finally kicked you out"
Aryann swallowed.
"I can guess why already. He got tired of your prudish attitude, then again, no one wants to be with you, Aryann" She mocked
Aryann's eyes narrowed and her face flushed with anger. Was that really it? She quickly shook her head, she shouldn't let Nicole or Luca ruin her first day at work.
"You're just curious to know what happened in his house, but you know.. I can't waste my time talking to you" She fired back and shouldered pass Nicole then stopped and turned around.
"And please Nicole, if we ever run into each other again and you don't have anything meaningful to say to me, don't even dare speak to me!" She warned and walked away leaving Nicole feeling so shocked and humiliated.

Almost an hour later, Aryann was sitting on the chair in her desk, she was glad most of the employees were around already, her face was numb from smiling.

"Hey, can you please send a........."

The man's words were cut off when she lifted up her head.

"Cole" Aryann bit out, surprised.

"You're the new receptionist?" Cole asked in disbelief.

"Yes, do you work here?"

"Yeah, I'm the manager and I can't believe I'll be seeing your face every morning" Cole replied, smiling broadly.

Her lips quirked but the smile did not get up to her eyes.

Cole stared at her from her head to her toes in sheer masculine admiration. He wasn't sure of many things in his life but he was sure of one thing.

'This has to be the power of destiny'

Aryann walked out of the company. Her first day had gone pretty smooth, well except the part of meeting Cole again, she still couldn't believe that they were working in the same place, she was slightly glad that she'd have someone to talk to at work but she didn't want to start anything romantically with him and she hoped he wouldn't want that too.

A red sport car pulled up beside her.

Cole got down.

"Mind if I give you a ride?" He asked.

"I'm good. My place isn't that far from here" She politely declined.

"C'mon, Aryann, I insist."

"I........."

"Please" He pressed on.

Aryann sighed," Fine."

She got into his car, he slid in too and drove off.

He had turned on a music titled "I hate you, I love you"

Aryann felt the lyrics was directly saying what she felt. When she couldn't stand it any longer, she spoke,

"Can you please turn off the music?"

"Sure"

Cole glanced at her, he wanted to start a conversation, he wanted to know if Luca was out of the picture.

"I don't mean to pry but are you and Luca still a couple."

"No"

'We were nothing' She thought.

Cole sighed relieved.

"You know…. when I got home that night, I couldn't stop thinking about you being with someone like Luca"

"Is there anything wrong with that?" Aryann asked, curiously.

"No…. nothing, it's just that, you guys don't look good together, c'mon he's Luca Anthony Herron, you need to see the women who flock around him, I know you ain't that kind of woman who wants his money, but he's not good enough for you"

"He's good enough for me, he was nice to me, I know I can never be like his sophisticated women but I can try, if only he wanted me, is something wrong with me, Cole?" She asked, desolately.

Cole saw her lips quiver, he knew she was going to cry. He quickly pulled over.

"There's nothing wrong with you, Aryann" He said, soothingly.

"He said I was beautiful, he said he had a good time with me, why….why couldn't he love me, I can't stop missing him… I want to be with him…."All her pent up emotions came crumbling down as tears rolled down her cheeks. He moved closer to her, not knowing what else to do, he pulled her into his arms, cradling her close as she shuddered against him.

He murmured soothing words to her and stroked her hair, hating himself for noticing how soft they were and her lovely scent.

What kind of man lusted after a woman when she was quaking in his arms with a broken heart?

"It's okay, Aryann" He said, lowering his voice to a gentle pitch.

She clung to him, rasping for breath.

As the tears kept coming, thick and fast, Cole wondered how she met Luca in the first place. What would have happened if he hadn't gone to study in Washington? would they still be together? Well, that didn't matter now, she was broken and vulnerable and he would use this opportunity to win her over.

An hour later, they were in Aryann's apartment, he had wanted to come in for coffee.

"Sugar or cream?" She asked.

"Black"

She nodded just as she'd expect from a man like him.

"I'll be right back" with that, he walked away.

Cole sat on the couch, he stared around, the living room wasn't big but it was comfy and warm.

Aryann removed two mugs from the cabinet, she measured the ground and filled the coffee pot with water.

As she waited on it to brew. A face crawled into her head, this was how he loved his coffee too, she recalled the mornings she would walk into the dinning room and see him drinking coffee, there was one time, he had shot her a smile and she had felt so giddy.

Cole stared at Aryann as she walked in with two mugs. She sat beside him and handed him a mug.

"Thank you" He blew on his coffee for a moment then took a sip.

An awkwardness, thick and unsettling cloaked the room.

"How was your stay in Washington?" She asked, not that she was really interested in knowing, she just wanted to kill the boredom.

"Well, it was nice but as they say, there's no place like home, I studied most of the time and……"

"You mean to say you didn't hang out, go clubbing and date?"

Cole chuckled." I went clubbing few times, and I dated twice but I guess no one can be like you, Aryann" He said in an attempt to make her blush but fails miserably.

"What about you? How was college?"

"It was okay I guess but I didn't have any time to be social , I worked part time"

"Knowing you so well, you wouldn't have gone to any party even if you were invited, you hated parties"

Aryann laughed." And I still do"

"How did you meet Luca?" Cole asked, curiously.

"I don't wanna talk about it"

"You seem to love him alot, was it a fairytale meeting you had?"

Aryann swallowed," Far from it"

"Then why do you love him?"

"Cause he's Luca. At some point, he'd always make me laugh, he makes me feel special, feel appreciated and unique. I guess I got too attached to him because I had never been so happy"

Cole moved closer to her" Aryann, another man can make you feel ten times more than all the things he made you feel, a man who deserves you wouldn't let you cry a single tear, he would want to be with you too" Cole said, softly. He wanted his words to affect her badly.

He stared at her beautiful brown eyes, her raspberry-ripe lips and her body that made him want to bury himself into desperately. Desire ran through him like hot lava.

He cocked his head and moved more closer to her, wanting to taste those lips.

Aryann gulped, this was what she needed, she needed to forget about Luca and move on.

"You feel so good around me"

"I'm the only one who can make you feel this way"

"Embrasse-moi"

Shutting her eyes closely, she could picture his face as he told her those words. She quickly stood up from the couch.

"I'm sorry" She muttered.

Cole ran a hand through his hair realizing that it might be hard to win her over but he wasn't giving up.

"It's okay and I better get going, you should get some sleep" He replied standing up, she quietly saw him off to the door.

"Goodnight, Aryann, you can dream of me, okay" He said, sweetly.

She forced a smile out of her," Goodnight Cole" She replied and closed the door then leaned against it, she came sliding down until she was on a sitting position, she hugged her knees up to her chest.

"I miss you, Luca"

"Luca finally let go of Aryann" Nicole announced walking into the living room.

Abruptly, Edward turned to face her." What the hell?"

"Where did you see her, Nicole? how is she?" Susan asked, curiously.

" She rented an apartment at 57's street. She seemed okay to me and confident, she even talked back at me, she used to be scared that Dad might hurt her if she talks back, I guess she really isn't coming back here"

Edward's teeth clenched, he needed Aryann right now, Luca couldn't have sent her off with nothing. He must've have given her a large amount of money, and that money should be his.

"I think I should visit her, I don't know…….I wasn't very nice to her and now that she's gonna be living far from us, I just want to apologise." Susan said.

Edward smirked." Yeah, you should. She's still your daughter anyway" He added.

Susan and Nicole stared at him quite surprised at his words.

Edward nodded positively, this had to work, he wanted Susan to visit her so she could confirm if Aryann is living comfortably, if so, the girl had to pay her debt.

"Good morning, beautiful" Cole said, walking up to Aryann's desk.

She looked around, the last thing she wanted was people thinking that she was dating Cole, he was quite popular among the women in the company. Relieved, that no one was close by, she turned to face him and smiled.

"Good morning" She replied.

"I wanted to take you out this evening on a date, please say yes" He requested.

"I can't go out on a date with you, Cole"

"Fine, let's not call it a date, what about a nice dinner of two adults getting to know more about themselves" He suggested.

"Still, I can't……."

"Do you want me to call my colleagues so we could beg you to go out with me?"

"Cole" She groaned.

Just then, he saw two of his colleagues approaching, a man and a woman.

"Hey! Please……"

Aryann quickly covered his mouth with her hand and felt her chortled against her palm.

She quickly took her hand away.

"You don't take no for an answer, do you?"

Cole smirked." I don't"

"Fine, I'll go out with you, Cole" She agreed, reluctantly.

"Thanks Aryann, I'll pick you up at six" And then, he walked off.

Chapter nine

"I want you to….to remember this day, we could go on other dates but this one is so special to me, by our next date, I'll be a better milonguero for you"
His words reverberated inside her head. Was the date really special to him?
"Liar" She muttered.

Luca and Harry walked into a restaurant.
"I can't believe I came here with you, you're so persistent" Luca complained sitting on a chair.
Harry sat down opposite him.
"You needed some air, Luca, this is good for you, and the sooner you pull yourself together the better for you" Harry warned.
"I'm perfectly fine, didn't I go to work yesterday?"
"Who didn't come to work yesterday is a hundred times better than you. You were in each meeting yet I had to explain everything that was said over and over again. I know this is hard for you, you don't feel whole but this pain would pass, you've worked so hard for years to build your companies, you can't keep losing focus like this"
"I just miss her so much, I wish I can see her again, even if from afar, even for just a few minutes" Luca muttered, feeling so exhausted.
"That's not gonna happen anytime soon but you have to get over her, first, let's stop talking about her and let's have a good time here, now, where the hell is a fucking waiter"
Harry looked around, he saw a waiter taking orders for a table. His eyes narrowed recognizing the lady and she was with a man.
"Fuck!" He bit out.
"What?" Luca asked.
He quickly turned to face Luca." Let's get outta here!"
"After dragging me all the way here with all the sermons, you just want me to leave like that"
"Luca, listen to me, we have to go, I just figured out that I hate this restaurant, it's no fun but there's one close………"
"Why do you seem so frantic, call a waiter, I'm getting hungry" Luca snapped.

"Luca….."

Seeing that he wasn't ready to call a waiter, he looked around, his eyes darted passed a table then quickly scurried back.

Aryann?

He had wanted to see her again but at least not with a man and definitely not fucking Cole.

Shit! He didn't know this kind of pain existed before. It was cutting his insides into shreds.

Was this the same woman who made him so happy few days ago.

She had said she wasn't in touch with Cole but just five days after leaving him, she's on a date with Cole.

"Liar" He muttered looking away from her.

"Should we leave?" Harry asked, he should've left Luca at home, it was way better than this.

"No" Luca replied.

He wanted to stare at her, just her and try to rid the image of Cole, he might not get this chance to see her again after this so he wanted to take in every inch of her body while he could.

He stared at her again, her hair was neatly packed in a ponytail, she had gotten more beautiful than the last time he saw her. Was she happy now? Did she even think about him at all…… even just a little?

Her lips curved into a smile, Cole was definitely making her happy. Cole had probably kissed her and made love to her.

A hard knot twisted in his chest and he felt momentarily winded at the image of Cole touching her……. Cole rising above her…….. Cole sliding inside.

Suddenly, her head snapped towards his direction, she looked damn surprised to see him and for an intensed moment, their eyes locked…

Luca was here? Just few steps away from her. She quickly looked away. Damn it! He didn't look his usual calm and collective self at all.

He looked disheveled.

Her eyes darted back to his table, he wasn't staring at her this time but was engrossed in a conversation with Harry.

Cole noticed Aryann wasn't listening to what he was saying, he followed her eyes and who he saw made him angry. He didn't bring her here to see the man she loves again, he brought her here so he could erase him from her memory.

"I think we should leave, Aryann" He suggested.

Aryann sighed. Seeing him was reminding her of their date, she didn't want that so it was best to leave.

Luca stared at her table again, they were leaving….

Harry glanced at her, something caught his attention, he recognized it because he and Luca had gone shopping for it. The bracelet…..She was wearing Luca's bracelet.

"Well, I know she cared about him, she was quite excited about the date and she obviously missed him when he traveled to France"

Maria's words reeled through his mind. He knew Aryann wasn't moved by material things, maybe it had some special meaning to her.

"You have to tell her, now" Harry said.

"I'm not telling her anything" Luca snapped.

"Don't be a coward, you have to tell her now, you might not get the chance again"

"I'm not a coward, you moron, she's on a fucking date and you want me to ruin it, she's gonna find me pathetic and vulnerable"

"It doesn't matter how she finds you, just talk to her, telling her how you feel will make you move on" Harry said, convincingly.

"Now, listen to yourself, you're speaking gibberish"

"It's not gibberish, Luca. Don't you wanna move on, don't you want this pain to go away, you'll keep feeling this way if you do nothing, you shouldn't expect a positive response though but just get it off your chest" Harry said, impatiently.

He smiled inwardly knowing that his words had gotten to Luca.

As Aryann headed to the parking lot with Cole, a part of her wanted to run back to the restaurant and beg Luca to love her too, but she quickly shook off that thought, it'd useless doing so.

She felt her hand being hold and effectively, she was twirl around. Her heart shook seeing the person standing before her.

"Can I talk to you for a minute?" He requested, calmly.

Cole teeth clenched. Seeing the look on Luca's eyes, he was damn scared that Luca wanted her back.

"Aryann, we have to go" Cole announced.

Aryann stared at Cole then Luca, he wanted to talk to her? About what? Whatever it is, she wanted to listen.

Cole saw that she wasn't going to say no to Luca, he had to say something, just anything to make Luca go away.

"How will you get home?"

Aryann saw pain etched on Luca's forehead and she backtrack.

"Home? you two live together?"

"No" She replied at the same time that Cole said yes.

Aryann turned to face Cole angrily.

"We don't live together" She reminded, sternly. Even if she didn't have anything going on with Luca, she didn't want him to think that she was living with another man.

"Aryann....you.....Ugh . Fine! I'll be waiting for you in the car" With that, Cole angrily strode away.

Aryann turned to face Luca, even as disheveled as he seemed, he was still gorgeous in his t-shirt and linen trousers, her belly tightened.

"You lied to me" He began, gruffly.

"About what?" Aryann asked, confused.

"You said you weren't in touch with him, and now you're on a fucking date with him!" He shot at her, fiercely.

"It isn't a date and I wasn't in touch with him, it just so happens that we are now working in the same place"

"You're working in the same place with Cole?" Luca sighed" I shouldn't have come after you, it was a terrible idea" He added and began to retreat.

"What do you wanna say to me?" She asked, curiously.

"Nothing" He snapped and turned around to walk away.

"Nothing? You can't certainly mean that, I..... I didn't mind that I was with someone else, I wanted to listen to whatever you have to say to me and it's nothing, you can do this, Luca..... I......."

He turned around to face her lividly." Stop acting as if you really want to hear what I have to say to you, aren't you happy now? You're with your dream guy, he's not gonna ruin you but me, I ruined everything, right?"

Aryann frowned." What are you talking about?"

"I tried.....I lied to myself that I wasn't falling, I thought I had shut down my emotions, I didn't want anyone to fool me into believing that I was in love, but it was hard to see you.....to touch you.......and not feel what's going on in my chest. You made me like this, Aryann. You did this to me just to turn me into a moron...... I've been a mess without you, I can't sleep at night cause I want you badly but I can't have you, I have been tempted to track you down and lock you up in my house but knowing that would only make you hate me more than you already do keeps breaking me apart."

Aryann just stared at him, speechlessly." Bu…..bu…..but you said I mean nothing to you?"

"I said that? When?"

"Earlier that day when you told me to leave, I had come by your study, I wanted you to watch a movie with me, you were on the phone with Harry and I heard that"

Luca rubbed his hand on his temple trying to remember what he and Harry had talked about. As the conversation trickled back into his head, he gasped.

"Fuck! I wasn't talking about you, it was Ava, Harry had said she was dating a business rival of mine to spite me, he asked if I didn't feel anything for her, that was why I said those things and I meant them"

Aryann thought about it, he didn't mention her name and she had just jumped into conclusion that he was talking about her, she couldn't believe she cried because that.

"Was that all you heard?" Luca asked, curiously.

She nodded.

"I had called Harry that day so he could tell me how to confess my feelings to you, you read so many fucking books and I wanted to be romantic for you. He suggested a candle light dinner, and we wanted to set it up the following day"

Feeling her blood rushed inside her veins with a giddily sweep, she was totally unprepared for this, she wanted to speak but Luca continued.

"You might not have noticed but I tried to give you space, the flowers and the date were to make you like me…. even just a little. I know, I was mean to you from the start, but I really hated seeing your tears and I despised myself for being the reason for it, that was why I let you go, you had cried that night, and if I kept on making you unhappy, I'll only be killing myself slowly."

"Wh…..what do I mean to you, Luca?" She choked out.

"Everything. Without you, nothing makes sense. I can't change what happened from the start but I was glad you came into my life, you completed me. I…. I…. I love you, Aryann. I know telling you this won't change anything but someone said it might make me move on. I know that's gibberish though but I feel kinda relieve saying this to you. I love you so much" He confessed, honestly.

Aryann felt a tug in her heart which threatened to explode with joy hearing him say these words to her.

He was retreating again….she couldn't let that happen, she quickly held his arm.

"Don't I get to say anything?"

"You don't have to" He snapped taking her hand away from his arm.

"I want to……."

"It's bearable that I already know how you feel about me, you don't have to remind me"

"You don't know anything." She retorted.

"I do….."

"I love you!"

Luca took a step back, did he hear that correctly." What?"

"I didn't cry that day because you were making me unhappy, I thought you would never love me too, you couldn't love Ava, so I never thought you would never like me……. I was happy……. with you, Luca…. I was more happy than I ever thought possible. I know we started off on the wrong foot and if anyone had told me before that I would come to love you this much, I wouldn't have believed. I can't forget about you, I don't want to forget about you" She confessed, showing him the bracelet.

Luca tensed, he had never thought she'd love him this much but she did and he suddenly felt he didn't deserve it.

"You deserve a gentleman, I'm not" He bit out.

She moved closer to him. Tears threatened and her voice hitched.

"I….. I need you, Luca"

"I can't control my temper" He reminded.

"We could work on that together" She suggested.

"I'm not romantic"

"I want you just the way you are"

She took his hand and placed it on her chest." My heart beats for you, Luca. I want to be with you

….. just you…… only you"

"Don't fuck with me, Aryann. I've given you all the reasons to walk away from me, you're not leaving and now I'm gonna love you insanely and I'm never letting you go, even if you run to the moon, I'll track you down, you're mine now, understand?"

She nodded happily." I love you, Luca"

And before she could say another word, his lips touched hers. Touched and sealed. Fire ran up her backbone. Fire…..and joy….and love. There was a warming in the pit of her stomach such as she had never felt before. Her eyes closed as the kiss grew hotter and deeper in seconds.

He took his lips away pulling in the needed air. He cupped her face and rested his forehead on hers.

"Don't show your lovely smile to any other man, my jealousy is bad" He warned.

"Don't look at any other woman too, you wouldn't want to see me being territorial, you know" She warned too.

Luca chuckled and kissed her again. She could feel him loosen her hair, so that it fell around her shoulders. Her world was reduced to delicious insanity. The touch and slide of his tongue against hers made her legs clench together to stop the pulse throbbing between them. Liquid heat was spreading outwards from the very core of her being. Their mouths moved over each other's hungrily. The long essence they'd had from each other fanned their desires recklessly.

The kiss lasted longer than he meant it to be, their lips seem unwilling to part company.

Harry leaned against the wall outside the restaurant smiling triumphantly.

Cole got into his car and drove off angrily.

Almost thirty minutes later, they were in her apartment, Luca looked around in pure disgust.

"My apartment's shabby, isn't it?" She asked.

"Yes it is" He replied.

Aryann rolled her eyes, did he really have to agree with that?

"You don't have to stay here any longer, go get your things!" He ordered.

"What....no! I'm not leaving" She retorted quickly.

"You don't wanna move in with me?" He asked in disbelief.

"There's nothing wrong if we live in different houses"

"Everything's wrong with that, you certainly don't want me to start telling you how I have been for the past five days, I want to see you when I wake up, I want you next to me before going to bed, don't you want that too?"

"I do but there's…….."

"I thought you said you love me!" He yelled startling her.

"I do and this isn't about……."

"You love me but you don't wanna move in with me, does that make any sense? how do you expect me to cope without you being in my house, it feels empty and I…. I just……fuck!" He yelled again.

Aryann stared at him surprised at how angry he was all of a sudden.

Luca knew two things were gonna happen if he remains here, he was gonna say hurtful words to her and break things in this apartment. That would only scare her away from him. He quickly turned around and walked off.

"Way to go, Luca. I'm proud of you" Harry said, sarcastically.
They were in Harry's house, Luca had just finished telling him what transpired between him and Aryann.
"She's so stubborn. Why can't she just agree with what I want?"
"Luca, I feel like punching life outta you right now, this is someone who we never thought could love you, and just when we find out that she truly does love you, you wanna make her think it was a mistake"
"But this is hard for me too"
"I know, but you have to stop thinking about what you want, you should also put her feelings into consideration, this is what she wants and you need to agree to this"
"What must I do to make her live with me again? Should I marry her?"
Harry frozed,"Take it easy bro, one step at a time, marriage is a lifelong commitment, you just got into a proper relationship with her, what you need to be doing now is to prove to her that you can be her dream guy, and walking out on her few minutes ago is far from it"
Luca sighed." I guess I have to agree to what she wants"
"Yes, and you really need to work on your anger issues, it's not getting better at all"
"Do you think I.... I can be good enough for her?" Luca asked, curiously.
"Yes, and you have me, together we'll groom you into a perfect boyfriend" Harry laughed.
Luca chuckled recalling the sincerity in her voice when she said he made her happy.
"And you shouldn't be making any mistake anymore, remember that guy at the restaurant, he seem so into her" Harry reminded.
Luca's fist clenched.
"Too bad for him, I ain't given up"
Harry patted him on the shoulder." That's my Luca"
Luca shot him a glare," Your Luca?"
"Stop glaring at people!" Harry snapped.

Aryann slowly lay down to sleep, she wished Luca hadn't gotten mad, she was already missing him.
"You love me but you don't wanna move in with me? Does that make any sense? How am

I supposed to cope without you being in my house, it feels empty and I…. I just…..fuck!"

He had seem so hurt saying those words to her. She saw nothing wrong with them living in different houses, they could visit each other from time to time, she wanted him to be okay with it too. Should she just move in with him? She stared at her cellphone, should she call him?

At that moment, her phone rang, seeing who it was, she quickly picked up.

"Hey" He began, calmly.

"Hi"

"Did I wake you?"

"No, I wasn't sleeping" She replied sitting up.

"I'm sorry for walking out on you earlier, I'm just not used to people saying no to me but I need to get use to it cause my woman is so stubborn"

Aryann grinned." Are you okay with this?"

"Ye….. yeah, if that's what you really want, …. I'm cool with it" He choked out.

Aryann sighed relieved.

"Do……do you still like me?" He asked, nervously.

"I love you, Luca, nothing can change that" She assured.

"Thank you, Aryann, I promise to work on my temper, it just isn't easy to change, but give me a few days, I'll change for you"

Aryann slowly turned on the light in her bedroom. She didn't want him to try to change so bad because of her, she just needed him in her life and that was more than enough for her.

"Why did you turn on the light?"

Aryann frozed,"Where are you, Luca?"

"Fuck! somewhere……"

She quickly jumped off the bed and opened the window then she saw him leaning against the door of his car across the road.

Gleefully, she ran out of her bedroom, she quickly slid into the flip flops she saw and raced out of her apartment.

Luca smiled seeing her running towards him, he was slightly frightened that she might fall, but then she jumped into his arms.

"Mine" He whispered stroking her hair.

She was on her nightdress and feeling every inch of her graceful body made his blood rushed to his groin.

She slowly disengaged from him.

"I missed you" She said.

"I can see that" He replied staring at her feet, she looked down and realized that she was wearing different pair of flip flops.

She smacked him playfully.

"It's your fault"

Luca chuckled.

"Are you really okay with this?" She asked.

"I have to be but you'll let me change the furniture's"

"Luca…….."

"I know you wouldn't want to move to a bigger apartment but at least let me change the furniture's, you're my girlfriend now, and as the girl of a super cool man, I want your apartment to look good not scary"

She smiled and covered her cheeks with her hands trying to hide the heat flaming her cheeks from him.

"I didn't say anything amusing" He reminded.

"You…..you called me your girlfriend" She said still smiling broadly.

Luca's heart leapt." It's not hard to make you blush. So will you let me change the furniture's?" He asked.

Aryann shrugged." Fine" With that she moved into his arms again wrapping her hands around his back, resting her head on his chest.

Luca smiled feeling so fulfilled.

"I want to be good for you, don't give up on me yet, Aryann" He whispered kissing her hair.

"I love you, Luca"

"I love you more, Aryann"

Luca strode into his house, Maria stared at him quite surprised at how lively he looked.

He sat beside her on a chaise lounge.

"Aryann and I are dating" He announced, excitedly.

Maria gasped." Really?"

"Yes" And then he told her all what had happened earlier that evening.

Maria smiled, she was happy for both of them.

"What do women want from their lover?" Luca asked.

"Well, in a relationship, I do believe it should be 50/50, both should try and make things work, women always want a man they can count on, who would make them their number one priority"

Luca stared at her for a while," Why didn't you get married? You can't certainly mean that you didn't have any man who loved you"

Maria sighed." I wasn't really lucky with love, Luca. And you know that I can't give birth, I've accepted my fate a long time ago and I'm happy with life"

Luca swallowed hard as he imagined how life would've been without Maria.

"Thank you, Maria for not giving up and leaving me" He said, sincerely.

Maria smiled, she couldn't remember when last she had seen Luca like this, so calm and happy. She moved closer to him.

"You ain't tryna hug me or some shit, right?" He asked staring at her suspiciously.

"Oh don't be a killjoy" Maria snapped and hugged him tightly.

Luca smiled, and slowly pulled away.

"That's enough hugging"

"If it were Aryann, you wouldn't say so"

Luca chuckled." Are you getting jealous?"

"Why would I? Aryann's like a daughter to me"

Luca frowned." If she is like a daughter to you, then who I am to you?"

"Now, someone's getting jealous" Maria teased.

Luca scoffed." You wish" And then he stood up, he bent and kissed her slightly grey hair.

"Goodnight, Maria" With that, he walked away.

Maria stared at him as he walked away. Who would have thought Aryann would turn Luca into this man? If there were to be a next life, she wanted to be his mother.

Harry and Luca walked out of the conference hall in his company.

"It's great to see you back to your normal self"

"I was always myself" Luca corrected.

"Seriously? Have you suddenly forgotten how broken you were when she left you, you even cried" Harry reminded.

"Me? I didn't cry, something flew into my eyes"

Harry gasped," I can't believe you're denying this"

"I can never....."

"Fine, I don't wanna argue with you right now especially not what I saw with my two eyes"

"Your eyes are bad" Luca teased.

"And you suck at lying" Harry slammed back.

Luca sighed" Do we really have to argue about this?"

Harry shrugged." I can never win against you even when it's the truth……so last night, I read some books, and I realize that some women love listening to love songs"

Luca stopped walking and turned to face Harry.

"Meaning?"

"Sometimes, you have to sing for her" Harry suggested.

"I can't fucking sing, my voice…….."

He was cut off when Harry burst into laughter.

"When I thought about it last night, I couldn't stop laughing, it'd be like listening to a frog" Harry mocked still laughing.

"Ha…ha" Luca remarked, sarcastically.

"My voice isn't that bad and it's definitely not a frog-like voice, I'm gonna prove you wrong, dick. Now tell me the love songs you know"

Harry shrugged then brought out his cellphone.

He played a song titled "Rewrite the stars" by Mac Efron and Zendaya.

As Luca listened for a while, he got irritated by it.

"This is a fucking break up song" He yelled.

Harry frowned." I think it's cool…."

"There's nothing cool about it, imagine,' fate's pulling you miles away and out of reach from me'

You've got to be fucking kidding me, you want me to sing this Godforsaken song to Aryann so she'll start having second thoughts about us"

"It's just a song, Luca, why are you getting angry at me, I didn't write it" Harry reminded.

"Send me the songs on your fucking phone, I'll be the one to choose" Luca snapped.

Harry shook his head and grabbed Luca's phone from him." You really need to loosen up"

"It's a break up song!" Luca declared.

Harry shrugged, Luca phone started ringing.

"Pretty whoa is calling" He announced, smiling sheepishly.

"I can't pick her calls right now"

Harry frowned," Why?"

"She's so pissed at me"

"Is making her angry your new hobby?" Harry asked, angrily.

"No, I didn't do anything that bad this time, don't worry, we'll make up together" Luca assured.

Harry sighed and continued sending Luca some songs.

Aryann heard a knock on her door, she walked up to her door and opened it.

"About time" She began.

Luca sighed." It's nice to see you too, baby" He replied walking into her apartment.

"Don't baby me, you said you wanted to change the furniture's, you changed everything, the bed, the kitchen cabinets, the couch, the curtains……."

"Woah! Did I do all that?" He asked looking around.

Aryann eyed him." You didn't call yesterday and you didn't pick my calls"

"Well, I knew you were gonna try to talk me into telling the workers to go away"

"Still, I wanted to hear your voice" She blurted out," Didn't you miss me?"

Luca smiled," Of course, I did……"

"Don't smile, I'm still angry"

Luca nodded suppressing his lips in a tight line" At least, your apartment doesn't look scary anymore, and you think this is easy for me, this long distance relationship?"

"Long distance relationship?" She asked in disbelief." it's just a twenty minute drive from your house to this place"

"As far as we are not living in the same house, it's long distance to me…. I'm sorry for not calling but I came to spend the night with you unless you don't want that" He announced.

She stared at the briefcase in his hand, her heart gladdened knowing that she wouldn't be sleeping alone tonight.

"I want you here,Luca" She admitted.

He smiled triumphantly." If you had said no, I'd have begged to stay"

"That doesn't mean I'm okay about what you did" She snapped.

He pulled her into his warmth embrace.

"Can't you just agree with everything I do?"

"Fine, it's not like I can change anything now, but the workers were quite cold, you know"

"I'm happy they kept to their words" He blurted up.

She lifted up her head to look at him.

"What did you do, Luca?"

"They were all men, I only told them not to look at you talk less of speaking to you if they don't wanna be jobless forever"

"Luca" Aryann groaned.

"I did pretty good, right?"

Aryann sighed heavily." Good doesn't fit in at all"

Luca shrugged." Anyway, let's forget about that and enjoy the evening, please"

"Okay"

"First let's go grocery shopping" He suggested.

"I have……."

"Can't you just say yes for once?" He grunt.

Aryann chuckled.

They slowly walked home from the mall, hand in hand, fingers entwined. Aryann stared at his other hand, he was clearly battling with the shopping bags.

"Can I help you with some……."

"No, it's fine, I'm a gentleman, my lady shouldn't carry things about" He replied knowing too well that her cheeks were getting pink already.

"We should've taken the car"

"No, I wanted to walk with you and we're almost home already?" He reminded.

'Home' Aryann thought, was it okay to picture a future with Luca?

"C'mon, I'll race you home" He suggested, excitedly.

"You think you can beat me with those shopping bags in your hands" She asked.

"I'm Superman" He joked.

She laughed and without warning, she ran off.

"I didn't even count!" He yelled and ran after her too.

Soon, he was ahead of her.

She quickly stopped running and held her stomach.

Luca glanced back, he quickly hurried back to her.

"Are you okay?" He asked, concerned.

"My stomach hurts, it must be something I ate" She replied and saw him dropped the shopping bags then she took off again.

Luca gasped staring at her as she ran off in disbelief.

"You cheat!"

At the end, he was waiting for her in front of the apartment building, he'd won.

Aryann walked up to him, breathlessly.

He smirked" After all the schemes, I still won, how do feel now, you little cheat"

"Damn! you are fit" She admitted, panting heavily.

"I know" He agreed, proudly.

"Are you sure you wanna cook dinner? Aryann asked for the umpteenth time.

"Yes"

"Have you ever cooked before?"

"No. I told you before that I'm good at anything I do so how hard can this possibly be?" He asked, proudly.

Aryann was scared of eating poison tonight.

"But…….."

"Go to the living room and watch a movie, don't watch any tragedy.

Chapter ten

"Go to the living room and watch a movie, don't watch any tragedy" He warned.

"Are you sure you don't need my help here?"

"No"

Aryann sighed and walked away.

Luca opened the kitchen cabinets and the refrigerator.

What should he cook?

Chicken soup?

No, might take too long.

Omelette?

No, might be too hard.

Pasta?

No, might be too…..hmmm….. whatever.

Noodles?

Yes! Noodles wasn't hard to prepare, right?

He quickly turned on the stove.

This had to be perfect.

Aryann stared at the wall clock, what the hell was Luca cooking?

The kitchen door opened and he walked out. He placed a flatware in front of her.

Aryann slowly opened the flatware.

She gasped." You spent almost two hours in the kitchen preparing noodles?" She asked highly surprised.

"I had to make sure it was perfect, now, try it" He suggested.

Aryann stared at the noodles, it didn't look appetizing at all.

She held a fork and tasted it, she felt like throwing up.

"How's it" Luca asked, curiously.

"Taste good" She choked out and with all her strength, she swallowed it without even chewing it properly.

"I know it would turn out great, this is the first time I've cooked for anyone so you should feel blessed" He said, proudly.

Aryann scoffed. He was acting proud over this….this….she didn't even know what name to give to the food.

"You should have a taste of it" She suggested.

"No, I want to watch you eat everything"

Aryann gulped. Eat everything?

"C'mon just have a taste" She coaxed.

Luca shrugged." If you insist" He walked over to the flatware and took a taste from it, immediately, his tongue registered the taste, he quickly ran into the washroom to throw up. Aryann laughed.

"Fuck! Did I cook that?" He asked walking into the living room again.

"Someone who said he's good at everything did" She replied.

"Uhg! Let's just say cooking is the only thing I'm partially good at"

"You're extremely bad at cooking. The noodles are overcooked, it's like mashed potatoes, let's talk about the tomatoes and onions, you didn't even slice them probably, they're as big as……"

"Can't you be a little bit encouraging? I never knew you were so good at tongue lashing people" Luca said, amused.

Aryann laughed and held her fork again.

"You ain't eating that" Luca said taking the flatware from her.

"But you spent a long time preparing it, I can manage……"

"No! You ain't eating it, do you think I would be okay if you end up having a stomach ache, let's just order for pizza" He suggested.

"What about Chinese?"

"I hate Chinese" He snapped but one look at her told him that she loves Chinese. Shit! Maybe he should try eating that soon.

He stood up to dispose the flatware.

"Mr chef" she teased.

"Mr chef's lady" He slammed back.

She giggled and he walked off.

☐

About five minutes later, the doorbell rang.

"The delivery guy is damn fast" Luca commented.

Aryann stood up and strode towards the door and she opened it, she frozed at who she saw.

"Hello dear" Susan began, smiling broadly.

"Is that the delivery guy?" Luca's voice sounded from the living room.

"Can I come in?" Susan asked.

Dimly, Aryann nodded wondering what Susan wanted from her.

Susan walked into the house, her mouth fell open taking in the sight of the apartment, it was simply lovely.

She was shocked to see Luca sitting on a couch, she thought he had let her go. He didn't look pleased to see her too.

Quietly, she sat on a chair. Aryann didn't know what to say to her, this was her mother for crying out loud, why does it feels like she was looking at a complete stranger?

Luca held her hand and pulled her to sit beside him.

"Mrs. Carson, It's being a while, what brings you here this late?" Luca asked trying to sound polite but fails woefully.

"I wanted to see Aryann and I certainly wasn't expecting to see you here"

"I can't be away from her, maybe it's one of the joy of having a lover"

"You two are dating?" Susan asked in disbelief.

"Yeah, I really do love your daughter, Mrs. Carson and I wouldn't want any negative vibes to come near her"

Susan swallowed. Now, she was a negative vibe?

"What do you want, Mother?" Aryann asked finally.

"I wanted to have a word with you.....alone" Susan drawled.

Luca frowned. There was no way he was......

"Luca, can you please give us a minute?" Aryann asked, softly.

His resolve crumbled." Are you sure you'll be okay?" He asked staring at her intensely.

"It's nothing, she's still my mother" Aryann whispered.

Luca sighed and pressed a kiss to her forehead then stood up. He shot Susan the "don't try anything funny" look then he walked away into the bedroom.

"What brings you here?" Aryann asked, calmly.

"I just wanted to see how you're doing and I guess......"

"Don't act as if you care, mom. Nicole probably told you she saw me and you wanted to see if I'm living miserably, right?" Aryann shot at her, harshly.

Susan's mouth thinned, Nicole was indeed right when she said Aryann wasn't scared of them anymore. She definitely couldn't talk to her like this before and she suddenly realized how much of a bad mother she had been to her.

"I'm sorry, Aryann. I know saying sorry would never change the story but I just want you to know that I truly am sorry for everything."

Aryann stared at her surprised. Did she mean her apology? She still couldn't help but think that Susan wanted something from her.

"I should never have despised you for what your father did to me, it wasn't your fault at all, I can't make up for lost times but I wish you'd still see me as your mother"

"You're my mother, nothing's gonna change that" Aryann replied, innocuously.

Susan smiled touched by her kindness.

"Luca seems to adore you, Aryann" Susan commented, honestly.

Aryann grinned. No one needed to tell her that.

"Believe it or not, I'm glad that you're happy with Luca and I hope it stays that way for a long time" And then she hugged Aryann.

Aryann slowly patted her on the back, she didn't know if she should be scared of this new Susan but she wanted to be in good terms with her mother.

"The pizza's getting cold" Aryann said walking into her bedroom, Luca hadn't returned to the living room since Susan left. He was sitting on the bed.

"What did your mother talk about?" He asked, gruffly.

She frowned wondering why he was being grumpy.

"Nothing much, she wanted to apologise for everything"

"Oh" He said, simply.

Aryann didn't like the way he was acting, he wasn't even staring at her but was staring at her cellphone.

"Cole called twice" He announced.

Aryann sighed, so this was what all this grumpiness was about?

"I didn't answer the phone though" He added placing her cellphone on the table.

"Luca, I……"

"Did Cole come into your apartment when you left me?" He suddenly asked.

Aryann didn't want them to talk about the past." He did"

"Did he make love to you?"

"God! He didn't, why would you think that? I haven't been with anyone since you" She retorted quickly.

"He didn't kiss you?" Luca asked this time meeting her gaze. He could see she was at a loss for words and the possibility that Cole might have kiss her made his chest ached.

"He did, didn't he?"

"No, but he tried to" She replied.

"Then what happened?"

"Luca, do we really have to talk about this?"

"Yes, what happened?" He pressed on.

"I couldn't kiss him cause I…..I suddenly thought about you, I wanted to be with you"

"Did you think about me each time you were with him?"

"Yes"

Luca sighed relieved.

"I still don't quite appreciate him calling you though and to think you two work in the same place, you're damn stubborn and you won't quit even if I ask you to, maybe I should have him fired instead"

"You can't do that, Luca!"

"I can do anything, the owner of KM finance wouldn't dare……"

Aryann quickly walked up to him and sat on his laps.

"You don't have to go that far, don't you trust me?" She asked staring into his eyes.

"I do but you can't certainly tell me that you haven't noticed that Cole is into you"

"I don't want anyone else, Luca….. only you" She whispered nibbling at his ear. She could feel his body hardening beneath her.

"You ain't playing fair, Aryann" He breathed.

She chuckled and knelt down between his legs.

Luca stared at her, amused.

She slowly undid his belt, he lifted his hips so she could pull off his pants and boxers.

She held his mighty erection in her hand and squeezed gently.

"Christ!" He hissed, momentarily forgetting about everything else.

After stroking life out of him for a few seconds, she finally closed her mouth around him.

Luca's eyes rolled back to his head as she sucked him.

"I'm the only man who you're permitted to do this with" He choked out.

"I'm the only man who can feel the pleasure of having your mouth around my cock" He shut his eyes as she took more of him into her mouth.

Fuck! He wanted to be deep inside of her so bad. He quickly pulled her from the floor as he slipped away from her mouth.

"What?" She asked.

"I want to kiss and stroke every inch of you"

His pulse sped up and his head slowly descended. He felt her breath feather across his cheek, adding fuel to his desire.

He covered her lips with his, she whimpered, straining closer to him as he deepened the kiss. Her lips yielded to him…..parted….He dipped his tongue inside, teasing hers into an erotic dance.

His hands roamed over her soft body, bringing her so close that she couldn't help but feel his desire. He couldn't get enough of her. He cupped her breasts through her shirt, gently squeezing the luscious weight in his hands.

"Oh, Luca" She breathed as her hands reached inside his shirt and caressed his chest. Her touch nearly drove him crazy.

His breathing was ragged." I want you, Aryann….so much."

"I want you too"

That was all he needed to hear, he made her lay on the bed and pulled off her shirt. He unfastened her bra, baring her breasts to his gaze, but then, he paused as if waiting for her to make the next move.

"Luca……touch me" She pleaded.

Luca savored Aryann's gasp when he cupped her full breast in his hand then lowered his head and took her nipple into his mouth. She cried out, sinking her fingers into his scalp. He grew more aroused knowing what he was doing to her.

He quickly moved down her body and pulled off her skirt and panties.

Without wasting any time, he took her clit into his mouth, his teeth gently grazing the bundles of nerves as he tongue worked on her folds. Her vision clouded with pleasure.

"Luca" She moaned out while his tongue assaulted her womanhood.

Luca sucked two fingers into his mouth staring into her eyes as he did so.

"Tell me what you want, baby" He growled softly rubbing tantalizing circles over her clit.

"Your fingers…. Please…. your fingers" She begged.

Luca's eyes clouded with lust as he plunged his fingers into her slick feminine folds. Giving her little time to adjust before pumping them in and out of her. She moaned loudly unable to keep to one position on the bed.

"Do you like that, Aryann, my fingers burried in that sweet little pussy?"

"Yes….Luca….Yes" She cried out, eyes fluttering as her orgasm drew near.

"Do you want my cock, baby?"

She nodded eagerly, he took his fingers away and rid himself off his shirt.

He quickly carried her up and bent her over the bed so her backside was to him.

He slid the tip of his manhood into her folds, he twisted her hair around his knuckles and pulled her closer to him.

He plunged into her, thrusting into her relentlessly. Her body moved with each movement he made.

His cock was stretching her open, something she could never get used to. Each hot slide of his Cock sent sweet and delightful sensations running through her body.

"Don't stop, please" She begged, breathlessly.

"I'm not stopping till you come undone around me, till I feel your walls tightening around my cock, I'm the only one who can do this to you Aryann" He growled.

"Whose girl are you?"

"Yours" She mouthed, her eyes rolling to her head.

"That's right, baby, now, tell me, whose man I am" He leaned down bending her head slightly and kissed her, his hips still bucking against hers.

"Mine" She grinned. Their eyes locked and as Luca had described she came undone around him, her walls tightening his cock triggering his own release. She cried out his name and he groaned loudly.

Slowly, they fell flat on the bed gasping for breath.

"I can't get enough of you, Aryann" He admitted.

She smiled and rolled into his arms.

After a few minutes, Luca covered them with the duvet, it was a perfect time to sing for her but he didn't want to look stupid so he turned her around so her back was to him.

"I wanna sing for you but don't look at me" He warned, sternly.

She tried to turned around but he wouldn't let her.

Aryann chuckled," Are you shy?"

"I'm not shy, why will I be shy? I'm Luca......."

"You don't have to explain yourself" She cut in, softly.

"Do you really wanna sing for me?" She asked, excitedly.

"Yeah but don't laugh" He warned and cleared his throat and started singing Ellie Goulding

"Love me like you do"

"You're the night, you're the light.

You're the colour of my blood.

You're the cure, you're the pain.

You're the only thing I wanna touch.

Never knew that it could mean so much...so much.

You're the fear, I don't care.

Cause I've never been so high.

Follow me through the dark.

Let me take you past our satellite.

You can see the world you brought to life…to life.

So love me like you do, lo-lo-love me like you do.

Love me like you do, lo-lo-love me like you do.

Touch me like you do, to-to-touch me like you do….

What are you waiting for?

Fading in, fading out.

On the edge of paradise.

Every inch of your skin is a holy Grail I've gotta find.

Only you can set my heart on fire…..on fire.

Yeah, I'll let you set the pace.

'cause I'm not thinking straight.

My head spinning around, I can't see clear no more.

What are you waiting for?"

She turned to face him but he quickly looked away.

"Why did you stop?"

"I tried, you think it's easy singing for you, I know you are already looking for ways to tease my voice" He snapped.

Aryann chuckled seeing his cheeks covered in deep shades of red, he was indeed shy.

Well, she wouldn't say his voice was great though, it was far from it but while he was singing, she had felt he was directly talking to her and the joy she felt right now was priceless.

She slowly rested her head on his chest wrapping her arms around him.

"Thank you, Luca for being mine" She whispered.

He slowly stroked her hair," You like the song?"

"I love it and I love you" She replied.

Luca smiled happily.

"Should I confess somethings to you?"

She lifted up her head to look at him" Things like what?"

"At the party, I had given you my jacket because I was jealous that some men were staring at your boobs, I had told you those jokes that day to make you laugh but you didn't even smile cause I suck at telling jokes and I broke your cellphone because you had Harry's number" He confessed.

Aryann stared at him shocked beyond words, he had fallen for her first? but he didn't even show it, he was damn good at hiding his feelings.

He slowly held her hand tracing a circle with his thumb." When I.....you know.... when I think about the way I treated you, I can't help but despise myself, I might not deserve you and I might not be good enough for you but I can try…….."

She pressed a finger to his lips." Stop trying Luca, you might just get tired of trying and realize that I'm not worth it"

He quickly took her hand from his lips." You're worth a thousand……."

"Luca, I just need you, I want us to stop going over the past, I love you for you, I don't want anyone else" She said staring at him intensely.

Luca smiled touched by the depth of her affection towards him.

"I love you, Aryann, so so much."

She smiled and rested her head on his chest.

Luca felt her hand wrapping around his cock.

"I'm not gonna sleep tonight, am i?"He asked smiling excitedly.

Aryann shot him a mischievous grin.

"Maybe"

He turned her over to lay spawl on the bed.

"You ain't wearing that to work!" Luca declared.

"I'm running late for work and this is the fifth outfit I've changed into this morning, what is wrong with this too?" Aryann asked angrily staring at her red pencil skirt and white long sleeves.

"Do you know how I feel right now, I wanna bend you over something and fuck you, another man might feel this way so I don't feel safe" He explained.

"You need to trust me, Luca" She snapped.

"I trust you but I don't trust any man, especially not when you're going around looking so beautiful" He retorted.

Aryann tried not to let his words affect her, this wasn't a time to blush but her cheeks were already heated.

"Where are your long skirts? I think you should wear one of those" He suggested.

"I'm not wearing any long skirt, you said no one wears those anymore"

"I take that back"

"Luca please, I'm running late for work" She reminded, agitatedly.

Luca sighed in defeat," Fine, I'll let you go but you have to spend the night in my house today" He requested.

Aryann smiled, she wanted to be with him too." Okay"

"I'll pick you up from work" And then he reached for her and pulled her against him, just before his mouth captured hers. She moaned and raised her hands to his shoulders and parted her lips to allow him deepen the kiss. By the time, he broke away he had trouble drawing air into his lungs.

"That's so you'll only be thinking about me today" He muttered, breathlessly.

By the time she finally got off work, she couldn't be more excited to see Luca. He had called that he was on his way already.

She walked out of the company, someone pulled up beside her and she recognized the red sport car to be Cole's.

He got down and strode towards her.

"You haven't been answering my calls, why are you avoiding me, Aryann?"

Aryann gulped, cole was nice but the last thing she wanted to do right now was hurt Luca, he clearly didn't like her associating with Cole and she knew she wouldn't be happy to see him anywhere close to Ava or any other woman.

"I don't think we have anything to talk about" She replied, calmly.

"How could you accept Luca back, can't you remember how hurt you were, how you cried in my arms, trust me, he's not worth any of this"

"You don't know anything about him and letting him back into my life is none of your business"

"Aryann, you're gonna regret this"

"Cole, what we had between us is in the past now, I want to be friends with you if only you want that too but if not, I won't appreciate you medling in my life"

Cole sighed." What has that man done to you?" He asked, angrily, he glanced passed Aryann and saw Luca getting down from his car. He knew he had no chances with Aryann now but he wanted Luca to show her that he'd always be a monster as people say.

"Fine, I guess I have to settle for the friend zone now, can't I at least get a hug from you?"

Aryann sighed relieved that Cole wouldn't try to make advances towards her again, at least now, Luca would have no reason to get jealous.

It was just a harmless hug right?

She slowly moved into his arms. Cole wrapped his arms around her burrying his face into her neck.

Luca's footsteps halted taking in what was just few steps away from him. Aryann was in the arms of another man? And fucking Cole for that matter. He tried to organize his thoughts, it was just a hug………it was just a hug. Fuck! Cole arms were around her body possessively.

Did his father always feel this way? Was that why he turned into a drunk? How could his father survive knowing that another man was screwing his wife.

Aryann wasn't even his wife yet but it was as if someone is trying to rip off his heart from his chest seeing her like this.

As he advanced towards them, he tried to think clearly, but his mind was vague……

"Hmmm" Luca cleared his throat announcing his presence.

Aryann broke away from the hug jerkily. The cold look in Luca's eyes made her tremble slightly. Damn it! She wasn't expecting him to see that, now, she felt so guilty, she should have just simply walked away from Cole when she had the chance.

"Oh…..hey Mr Herron" Cole began grinning sheepishly.

"I don't quite appreciate you hugging my lady, Charles" Luca said between gritted teeth.

"It's Cole" Cole corrected.

"Who's cares about your fucking name?" Luca snapped.

Aryann didn't like this tensed atmosphere at all, she quickly held Luca's arm.

"Let's go, please" She begged.

Luca removed her hand from his arm. He wasn't gonna be hotheaded about this, he had said he wouldn't let things get to him that much and he would do just that.

"I know how it feels to want something you can't have, you can't change that so you have to back off, she's taken."

Cole smirked." I know it's temporary, I mean I can't help but wonder what you want from Aryann, considering the women you could have, why Aryann? sooner or later, she'll realize that you two can never be good together and when that happens, I'll be…….."

Rage found its way through the powerful punch that sent Cole falling to the ground.

Panic seeped through Aryann.

"Luca stop!" She yelled.

As she tried to bend towards Cole who was wiping blood away from his broken lip, Luca grabbed hold of her wrist.

"Next time, don't fucking dare say shit to me, I could ruin your life in a heartbeat" Luca warned and strode away dragging Aryann in his wake.

His hand tightened around her wrist and she bit back a cry. When she could finally speak, she managed to get out.

"Luca….my hand… you're hurting me"

He finally stopped and she wrenched her hand away from his grasp, rubbing it. He slowly turned to face her.

"Isn't that what I'd always do?"

Hurt ripped through her chest realizing that Cole's words had affected him, badly.

He ran a hand through his hair in a frantic gesture and said curtly.

"You should go home…. your apartment I mean"

"But we…."

"Just go! stop acting stubborn, stop acting as if you're okay with me, you're fucking turning me into a fool and it's not funny" He yelled.

Aryann swallowed hard, they shouldn't talk right now, he was furious, not that she scared of him but he wouldn't listen to whatever she had to say right now.

She grabbed his car mobiliser from him and pressed a button, the car beeped. Without saying anything, she walked up to the car and got into the passenger's seat, she was spending the night with him whether he likes it or not.

As he drove off without even glancing at her, he was clenching the steering wheel so tight that his knuckles were turning white.

Aryann sighed staring at him, She concluded that Cole really deserved that punch, and she should have added to it.

Edward walked into his bedroom, he found Susan brushing her hair.

"You still haven't told me how Aryann's faring now" He began, sitting on the edge of the bed.

"I don't quite get it, are you really concerned about her?"

"Woman, don't act like a saint now, you think it doesn't sound silly that you suddenly care about her?"

"There's nothing wrong in patching things up with my daughter, even if I can't be a part of her life, I'm still glad that she's happy now, who would have thought that Luca would end up being her man?" She covered her mouth with her hand as soon as she said that, she knew how Edward would react, that was why she hadn't talked about Aryann since yesterday, now it was too late.

"Aryann and Luca are dating? "Edward asked, surprised.

Susan sighed." Yes and he seem to be really into her"

Edward smirked." That's good then"

He was happy with this new turn of events, he still wished he had given Nicole to Luca but he couldn't turn back time so he had to stick to his plan.

"Aryann is happy now because of me, She should be thankful"

Susan sighed, she tired of hearing that.

"Edward, why do you feel that Aryann's life should revolve around you? Fine, you took her in and I'm grateful for that, when we sent her off to Luca, no one expected this to happen, so stop feeling like she should be grateful to you all the time"

"I need money, Susan. She's the only one who can help me, didn't I inform you that the bank is coming for this house any time from now, my company's fallen, Luca is filthy rich and......."

"We can get through this without dragging anyone into this, fine! we can't stop the bank from taking our house but we can move to a smaller apartment, you can look for a job, I'll look for a job too, let's just......."

"I'm not starting from scratch when I can get help easily."

"What makes you so sure that she'll help you? We're talking about millions of dollars" She reminded

"She'll have no choice but to help me"

"Edward, don't do anything you might regret" Susan warned.

Edward stood up." Don't worry, I won't hurt her" He assured.

Edward walked into his study, he slowly slumped on his swivel chair, he ran a hand through his table, he couldn't be poor again, he had trampled on alot of people just to get to the top, now, he was falling again, and falling fast, he couldn't imagine himself living in a small apartment.

He reached out for a drawer and pulled it opened, a long knife glittered. It had been long since he used this, he didn't want to have any reason to use it on Aryann if only she would just comply.

"Christ! can't you and Luca get passed any day without quarrelling?" Maria asked after Aryann had finished telling her what had transpired earlier.

They had arrived home few minutes ago and he simply walked away into his study still giving her the silent treatment.

Aryann thought about the previous night when everything had seem so perfect, and the song, she knew Luca was trying his best for her and strangely it bothered her that he might just get tired of trying.

"It was just a hug, Maria, if I had known that it'd lead to something like this, I wouldn't have even talked to Cole" She said, ruefully.

"Well, how would you feel if you saw him hugging a woman who likes him and then she ends up reminding you of your biggest insecurity?" Maria asked, seriously.

Just thinking about that hurt.

"Now that I think about it, Luca had those rules before cause he was scared to end up like his father, he probably thought being in love was being under the control of someone"

Aryann's heart clenched hard thinking about what he had said to her, did he really think she would do something deliberately to hurt him?

"I have to fix this, do you think he would want to talk now?"

"Well, he has to and don't worry I'll be in my room, I won't interrupt anything" Maria assured.

Aryann's cheeks flushed realizing what Maria meant.

"We're just gonna talk"

Maria shrugged laughing." Who's saying otherwise?"

Aryann grinned.

Aryann slowly knocked on the door of his study.

No answer.

She bent the doorknob and walked in, she found him typing speedily at his keyboard.

"Can we talk?"

"No, I'm busy" He snapped staring at his monitor.

She moved closer to him.

"I... I'm sorry" She muttered.

But he wasn't giving her any attention at all.

"Just tell me what to do to make everything okay again, I'm so sorry, I know I can't change what happened earlier but it won't happen again"

His fingers retreated from his keyboard, he rested his back on his swivel chair still not staring at her.

"How was he like to you? What did he do for you?"

"Luca, that's a long time ago"

"Just tell me, he didn't hurt you….. not even once, did he?"

"I don't wanna talk about that"

"Just fucking answer me….."

"I liked Cole but I love you, it's two different feelings!" She yelled desperately trying to make him feel better of himself.

He finally stared at her.

"I can't get the picture of the two of you out of my head and it hurts…. I know I sound pathetic right now"

"No, I would feel worse if I were to see you like that in the arms of another woman" She confessed.

His features began to soften." You would?"

"Yes and I'm so sorry" She slowly held his hand.

"Please don't be mad" She pleaded.

Against his will, a smile lit up his face, he slowly pulled her into his laps.

"If it would make you feel any better, do you want me to look for a new job?"

"You would do that for me?" He asked touched.

"I don't want you to keep feeling insecured"

Luca recalled that Harry had once told him that women hate feeling controlled. As much as he would like to agree to this, he knew she loved her job.

"You don't have to do that"

"But……"

"It's fine, Aryann. I don't want you to quit because of me. I'm sorry for losing my temper, I really didn't want to act violent in front of you"

"Cole deserved that, he had no right to say that"

Luca grinned." Then I should've have broken his nose too" On seeing her scowling at him, he quickly added.

"I'm just joking"

She leaned into his chest.

"I'm sorry for raising my voice at you and asking you to leave, I didn't mean that, if you leave me, I won't survive"

She slowly sat up and stared at him.

"I don't want to imagine my life without you, I'm not leaving, I might sound clingy, but I'm going nowhere" She declared.

Luca smiled relieved and kissed her.

He was kissing her so hard and all she wanted next was for him to tip her to the table or the floor and take her but he suddenly pulled back.

She stared at him confused, he seemed disturbed.

"Are you okay?" She asked, concerned.

"yeah, just tired" He replied and pulled her into his body resting his head on her back.

Aryann's eyes opened, she looked around, she was alone in bed. She stared at the wall clock, it was 1:16am.Where did hell did Luca go to? A sound came from the bathroom, fumbling with the darkness, she managed to turn on the lights.

"Luca?"

No answer. She knocked softly on the door of the bathroom.

"Luca?"

A groan and a soft shuffle sounded from the other side of the door.

"Go back to bed" He said, hoarsely.

"Are you okay?"

"I... I'm just not feeling too well. I'll be okay, just go back to bed"

"Is there anything I can do?"

"Aryann" He groaned getting annoyed by her questions.

"I'm fine, just please go back to bed"

She sighed uncertainly and walked back to the bed, this was rare, she had never seen him ill before.

After a while, he walked out of the bathroom, he looked like hell.

"What's wrong?" She asked, worried.

"It's my stomach, I think it must be the Chinese junk I ate for lunch"

Aryann frowned." You hate Chinese" She reminded.

"You love Chinese" He slammed back slumping onto the bed.

"I don't get it"

"I wanted to have that in common with you"

Aryann's heart sank, he was sick because of her?

"Why would you want to have that in common with me?"

"Don't lovers need to have things in common?"

"We love tango" She pointed out.

"And?" He drawled.

"It doesn't matter, Luca. Do you think this is easy for me knowing you're pratically trying hard to make sure I'm okay with everything you do, this should be 50/50,I should make you happy too, and……."

Luca didn't hear what she said next but he snapped up his head to look at her noticing that she was gonna cry any moment from now.

"Okay, I won't do anything to make you worry anymore, now drop this issue, the last thing I want tonight is seeing those tears, you might just increase the ache in my stomach" He warned.

Aryann sighed deeply." No wonder you didn't take me in your study"

Luca smiled mischievously." You wanted me to take you?"

"Don't teased me"

"Well, I'm sorry I couldn't, if I did, I wouldn't have satisfied you well enough."

Aryann grimaced." what's that supposed to mean?"

"Hey, don't you know I focus so clearly when I'm thrusting in and out of you especially when you start screaming 'harder Luca, don't stop, deeper……"

She threw a pillow at him covering his face.

He laughed.

"I do not remember saying any of those things to you" She denied.

"How will you remember when you were far away in cloud nine?" He asked loving the deep shades of red enveloping her cheeks.

"My point here is that, I need to fuck you when I'm perfectly okay so that you'll be more than satisfied"

Aryann gasped." For someone who is sick, you sure have the power to talk about sex" And then, she stood up.

"I'm already getting better, you're my medicine"

Aryann smiled and headed towards the door.

"Where are you going?"

"You didn't eat dinner and I have to prepare something for you so you can take some pills" She replied.

Luca grinned and the word that slipped into his mind at that moment was 'wifey'

"Don't take too long"

She nodded and walked away.

He slowly rested his head on the pillow.

Almost an hour later, she walked into the bedroom, holding a tray, Luca lifted up his head, now he was starting to feel better realizing she had been wearing his shirt all along. He slowly sat up.

She placed the tray beside him and opened up the plates.

"Chicken soup!" He exclaimed excitedly.

Aryann smiled, she was glad that he was starting to look much better. He picked up the cutleries but she took them from him.

"I want to feed you" she announced.

Luca grinned." Someone's treating me like a baby"

"You're my baby"

Luca slunged her a mischievous smile.

"I'm now going to act like a baby" He announced.

"Start feeding me already" He ordered and she did so immediately.

"Water"

She quickly gave him water.

Luca pursed out his lips showing her the sauce on his mouth.

Aryann took an handkerchief and wiped his lips gently feeling his lips through the handkerchief.

"I'm still hungry" He pressed on and she continued feeding him.

"I'm full" He announced.

Aryann heaved a sigh of relief then quickly gave him some pills.

"Now, please sleep" She requested.

He moved closer to her and placed his head on her chest encircling his arms around her.

"Pet me"

Chapter eleven

Luca's fists ball at his sides and with all his might, he willed himself not to move.
Panic clawed upwards through his throat, her face showed results of Edward's fist, what the hell had he done to her before he got here?
"I don't know why you're doing this but please, you don't have to hurt her, I'm begging you"
Edward grinned amused." Will you just look at how the tables have turned…. Almighty Luca is begging. But I don't need your pleas"
"What do you want?"
Edward stared at Aryann, how much could he possibly want now? He knew that if he managed to get out of here, he would no longer be safe in this country, he had to act wise and with Aryann in his grasp, he would be able to leave the country before getting caught.
"I need money desperately and your lady didn't want to do anything that would hurt you, isn't that so sweet?"
Luca stared at Aryann, she was sobbing softly. He didn't know what to think right now and how to feel about this but he badly needed to stop those tears and he just didn't want to think about the possibility of living the rest of his life miserably without her.
"How much do you want?"
Edward smiled." Well, let's start with how much you are willing to give me right now?"
"Edward….. please"She pleaded in a hoarse voice.
A surge of pain swamped Luca and he dragged in a shaky breath.
"Aryann, everything's gonna be fine,you'll be okay….you trust me, right?"
She shakily nodded.
Edward laughed hysterically.
"Don't fucking lie to her before she dies"And then,he called out his account details for Luca.
"I can't just transfer….."
"Are you seriously trying to stall,Luca? Everything is possible when it comes to you, have you forgotten who you are already"He said bringing the knife more closer to her neck.
Luca hurriedly tapped on the keyboard on his cellphone.
"I hope you ain't texting anyone to call the cops?"
Luca quickly showed him the screen of his phone.
"I'm not"

As much as he would like to do that right now but if that knife slit through her throat,he didn't know what he'd do with his life.

Minutes passed and Edward heard his phone beeped.

He smiled and suddenly thought about how much he could get from Luca tonight.

If greed was a race,you'd surely find Edward at the finish line before anyone else.

"I want twice of what you just sent"

"But that was fifty million dollars!"

Edward replied by cutting a line on her chin.She whimpered struggling but his grasp tightened around her.

Luca's heart squeezed, seeing blood flowing down her neck.Damn!If he could get her out of Edward's hold,he would fucking kill him.

"Ed….. Edward, I'll do anything you want,please stop…. don't hurt her more than this"He pleaded, painfully.

Edward smiled.

"Power feels good"

He realized just how much she meant to him and he would use that to his advantage.

After a few minutes,his phone beeped again,a warning went off that he should find a way to get out of here but he pushed it aside.

"I didn't tell you to stop transferring more cash,did I?"He asked, sternly.

Aryann swallowed hard.Edward's greed had no limit and she didn't want to be the reason for Luca's downfall,she shakily looked around,she heaved a deep breath,she had to break free from his hold.

Gathering her strength,she stepped on his feet,he looked down at her temporarily distracted.

"Don't try anything funny"He warned, feeling his hand slightly tight on her wrist,she elbowed him hard on the stomach,he groaned and she fell to the floor.

Luca's cellphone slipped from his hand instantly and he lunged towards Edward,he swung his arm up and knocked at the knife in his hand,it fell to the floor.

Before Edward could do anything, Luca slammed his fist into his gut.Edward landed on the floor,he tried to shove Luca off his body but the latter balled his hand into a fist and punched him in the face.Blood spurted from Edward's nose and he spit out a curse but the image of her bruised face and injured chin taunted Luca and he punched Edward again.

Edward's head lolled to the side but fury made Luca punch him again and again.

"Luca stop….you're gonna kill him"Aryann cried.

"He should die!"Luca growled,still punching life out of Edward who thought he was already seeing the gates of hell.

"Luca….stop… please"She begged.

Luca's teeth clenched in defeat but he was slightly satisfied with the sight of Edward's bloodshot eyes and damaged face.

He stood up from Edward's body and hurried over to Aryann.

Her forehead immediately fell against his chest, and he felt her shoulders shaking,she was trembling as a sob escaped her.

Luca cradled her close.

"It's okay, you're okay now"He murmured, soothingly.

She slowly nodded against his chest and he pulled her back, tipping her chin to look at the cut Edward had made.

The thin crimson line was still bleeding slightly, guilt weigh him down for not being able to stop this from happening but she wasn't in Edward's grasp again and that was bearable.

"We should go to the hospital"He said, concerned.

"I'm fine… I just want this night to end"She replied and hugged him again.

Luca slowly stroked her hair, whether she likes it or not,she wasn't going to live apart from him anymore.

Edward slowly sat up,his life couldn't just end like this,he had money now,he just had to get out of here,he felt like hell,he knew even without a mirror that Luca had ruined his face.Lividly,he looked around and saw his knife.He quietly reached for it.

Luca thought he heard footsteps,he turned around abruptly just to feel a knife piercing into the side of his stomach.

He gasped and stared at Edward who smiled triumphantly and pulled out the knife.

"No hard feeling Luca, except that one"With that,he dashed out.

Luca fell to the floor, Aryann bent towards him,tears already streaming down in thick sheet.

"What….. I…..you….."She choked out unable to form a sentence.She frantically got her phone and called an ambulance.

When she came back to him again,she ripped off the bottom of her dress, tore a section from it and folded it to press over his wound to stem the blood flow.

He groaned holding his stomach and her uncontrollable tears wasn't helping matters.

"Aryann…..stop crying…. I'll be …fi…. fine"He pleaded between gasp.

She stared at his trousers,it was getting soaked with blood,he was really losing alot of it.

Heart hammering double time,she choked out.

"Don't leave me,Luca" She crawled next to him making his head rest on her chest.

He tried to speak…..to tell her that he wouldn't dare….but pain was rocketing through his body, and as hard as he tried to fight the darkness, everything went blank.

His eyes opened,a bright light made him shut them back,he groaned and dimly heard footsteps.

"Finally"He heard Harry's voice exclaimed.

He slowly opened his eyes,he was lying on the bed,he felt a sharp pain on the side of his stomach.

"You have no idea what I've been through trying to calm two women down for the passed two days,they should know you better by now that you don't know when to give up"

"I've been out for two days?"Luca asked, weakly.

"Yeah, how are you feeling?"

"Terrible…… where's Aryann?"He asked then noticed Harry suddenly acting uneasy.

The door opened and he looked up expecting to see her but it was Maria.

"Luca"Maria squealed and ran towards him.

She was wanted to hug him but Harry came to his rescue.

"He's still very weak"

"Oh"And then she held his hand.

"I'm so glad that you're awake"She said with tears filled eyes.

Luca sighed."Where's Ary……"

A sound came from the door,he looked up expectingly but it was the doctor.

"It's so nice to see you awake,Mr Herron"

Luca just nodded curtly.

"Thankfully, the cut wasn't that deep to affect any major organs so you'll be okay soon,we just have to watch you for a week"The doctor announced placing him on another drip.

"A week? I'm okay,doc. I can go home tomorrow"Luca snapped trying to sit up but a surge of dizziness made him lay right back.

"He'll do as you've said"Maria assured.

Luca stared at the hospital gown on his body."Who the heck wore me this ridiculous outfit, I look like a clown"He complained, angrily.

"Who complains about hospital clothes after surviving a knife wound?"Harry asked.

Maria chuckled."Luca"She replied.

"It's high time you have this ridiculous outfit changed into something fancier"Luca scolded.
The doctor shrugged.
"Yes sir.And please don't try to move for the meantime, your wound might open up,it would be a big problem if it gets infected"With that, the doctor walked away.
"Would someone finally tell me where the hell is Aryann?"
Harry sighed."She left almost an hour ago when the doctor had informed us that you'll be waking up any moment from now"
Luca gasped."She left?She doesn't want to see me?"
Maria slowly sat on the bed.
"She wouldn't stop blaming herself for what happened"Maria replied.
"But she didn't do anything"Luca said getting frustrated.
"I tried telling her that but it was damn hard convincing a weeping lady to think positively I guess she's just still shocked at seeing you getting stabbed in front of her."Harry said.
Luca let out a breath he had been holding."What about that old crook?"
"We were really lucky,the cops caught him,he almost left the country.His company has completely fallen, the bank are going to seize his house,that was why he wanted Aryann's help, Susan said he had talked about approaching her but she didn't know he would go this far,I got your money back"Harry explained.
"We should settle things with the bank so that his family can keep his house, Susan is still her mother but that scumbag has to rot in jail"
"Definitely"Harry agreed."And after you've gotten better,you should try to talk to Aryann, I've put my all in securing this relationship and it has to work"Harry added.
"I'm not waiting till I get better,you'll have to get that ring I chosed online right now"
Harry frowned."You want to propose to a lady who thinks she brought badluck to you,she might not agree right now,you have to....."
"Get me that ring right now and you Maria.....you have to make her come here"
Maria shook her head."She won't....."
"Tell her I died or something"
Maria frozed."I'm not telling that kind of lie, it's scary and might just give her a heart attack"
"Just tell her anything"Luca snapped, agitatedly.
"Fine"Maria agreed bringing out her cellphone.
Harry stared at him,well, nothing could change Luca's mind now.

Aryann got down from the cab, Maria had called to say Luca had woken up but his health kept deteriorating and he wouldn't let the doctor attend to him saying he would get treated when she comes to see him

Her mind was in a tangled knot covered in guilt but she wouldn't be able to take it if she lost him completely.

She hurried into the lobby.

"Aryann"She heard his voice called weakly.She slowly turned around to see him sitting on a couch.He looked pale but based on Maria's description,she wasn't expecting him out of bed already.

"Aren't you supposed to be in bed?"She asked, calmly.

Luca stared at her intensely,God!He wanted them to get passed this moment and forget anything like that ever happened as he stared at the dark circles under her eyes,her already healing bruises and the bandage on her chin.

"I am, but what do you expect me to do when you don't want to see me"

"It isn't like that,Luca.I was so scared that you could've died, I just wouldn't be able to take it, and it's all my fault"She said tearfully.

"I didn't die and nothing was your fault, Edward did all those not you and I definitely didn't get stabbed because you, he's just insane"

"Even so,that would leave a scar and each time you look at it,it would remind you of that night,and you might regret everything"

"I know we won't easily forget about that day,but we need to get through this together,do you think leaving me is what's best for me?"He asked and she could see pain etched on his forehead.

"You said before that you were scared to let me go and you are just going to give up on me now that I need you most?"

She swallowed,she hadn't really thought about how he might feel about all this,he still needed her, wasn't that enough reason to try and bury this guilt?

"I'll never give up on us, Aryann,not now….not ever"He declared and brought out a ring box.

He slowly opened it.

She gasped.

"I know this might not be the right time for this but I can't wait any longer to make you my wife, I admit I have so many flaws, but I want to be the best person in your life,I wanna ride happy moments with you,I know we might have our differences but I want us to be able to sort things out together…… Let me give you the world, Aryann…. please marry me and make me more happy than I ever thought possible"He requested, desperately studying the expression on her face,she seemed at a loss for words.Maybe he wasn't doing this properly.

He went down on one knee trying to bare the pain in his stomach.

"You shouldn't be......."

"I'm fine,I can handle anything"He cut in softly and stretched forth the ring to her.

People stopped on noticing the scene and Luca knew that Aryann was going to be popular after this,what if she says no?

"I want to be with you..... only you.... from dusk till dawn.. I would read those fucking novels to you and I'll watch those miserable movies with you"

Aryann laughed through her tears.

He was glad to hear his favorite sound again.

"Please Marry me, Aryann"

"You might regret this"

"I want to spend the rest of my life with you, that's the only thing I know right now"

"It might get boring"

"Marry me, Aryann"She could see tears flooding his eyes.

She tried to stem her tears,she looked down at him and smiled,she didn't know if she deserved this man but she knew if she let him go,she would regret it for the rest of her life.

"I'll marry you, Luca"She choked out amidst tears.

He smiled joyfully,he heard coos and applauds around them.

'People can't seem to mind their business'He thought and sat down again noticing the pain he was feeling had increased.

She sat beside him and he slipped the ring into her finger,he slowly kissed her knuckles.

"How does a honeymoon in Paris sound?"

She smiled."sounds perfect"

He cupped her face and smoothed his thumb across her cheeks wiping her tears.

"That's the last time I wanna see those tears"He warned and held her hand, lacing their fingers together.

"Promise me that you'll grow old with me"

She moved closer to him,"If it meant that I met you,I'd choose this life over and over again, I'm not going to think of giving up on us again, nothing is worth giving this up for"And then she kissed him deeply,he reciprocated almost immediately and instantly she knew that the current of love and understanding that flowed through them could never be disrupted.

He pulled back and rested his head on her shoulder.

"You might wanna call Harry to bring me the wheelchair"He announced.

She shakily stared at his stomach and saw blood,his wound had opened up.

"Luca"she groaned.

Luca chuckled despite his pain knowing that she wasn't the only one who would scold hell out him,he would also have to go through Maria…. Harry….and the doctor.

But that didn't matter now,he had his queen with him and right now, everything seem lighter and brighter.

NEARLY SIX YEARS LATER………

"Morning Maria"Luca grunt walking into the dining room.

Maria turned to face him.

"You look a mess"She teased.

He opened the refrigerator and took a bottle of water.

"Don't tell me about it"And then he gulped down everything in the bottle.

"Did Aryann have one of those hilarious dreams again?"

"Uh-huh, and last night was worse,she practically wept that I called her fat in her dreams and after I could manage to calm her down,she wanted to eat waffles,She ate lots of it just to end up crying again that I see her as a glutton,is that fair, Maria?"Luca asked.

Maria laughed."You did appear in her dreams though.Have you been giving her any reason to think that way?"

"First off,I can't control dreams and my real self wasn't in that dream, second,She isn't getting fat, except for her baby bump which keeps getting bigger, she's still damn sexy,why can't she get that?"

Maria shook her head."You two are one of a kind"

"I can't wait for her to give birth and she won't take in again"He declared.

"Morning Dad…Morning Grandma"Four years old Damian greeted sitting on a chair.

Maria grinned joyfully,it meant so much to her when Luca had told his kid to call her grandma, and even after hearing that so many times,she could never get used to it.

"Buddy,did you sleep well?"Luca asked.

"Yeah"

"Did you brush your teeth?"Maria asked.

"I did.Is mom still sleeping?"

Luca wished she was.

"No, I'll go get her for breakfast"With that,he walked away.

Luca walked into his bedroom, scratch that, their bedroom.He found her putting a shirt on.

Unconsciously, he ran his tongue over his bottom lip taking in the sight of her naked butt.

"Don't even think about it, I'm hungry"She said pulling a short up to her waist.

Luca sighed,she was six months gone already,he wished he could fast forward time and at the same time,he was scared of the day she would put to bed.

"Breakfast's ready"He announced and turned to walk away.

"You ain't gonna carry me?"She asked, surprised.

Luca turned to face her.

"You always complain each time I offer to carry you since you took in"He reminded.

"But I always agree at the end, right? women need to put up a show at first and then agree"

Luca huffed."You never sieze to amuse me everyday"And then,he strode towards her and carried her in bridal style.

She smiled,"Am I heavy?"

Luca stared at her smile fading already,he wasn't ready for this again.

"Don't start please"He begged.

Few minutes later,he lowered her on a chair in the dinning room.

She had already exchanged pleasantries with Damian and Maria.

"So Aryann, did you sleep well,Luca told me you had a bad dream?"

Luca frozed avoiding Aryann's eyes."You ain't supposed to tell her anything"He mouthed.

Aryann shot him a death stare.

"You had a bad dream mommy? what was it about?"Damian asked curiously.

"Someone hurt my feelings"Aryann announced.

Luca rolled his eyes dramatically.

"Someone hurt you? weren't you scared?"Damian pressed on.

"Of course she wasn't, Daddy was right there beside her and got rid of the obnoxious dream from her mind, don't you know who I am?"

Damian giggled."You're Superman and I'm Superboy"

"My ass"Aryann mouthed.

Maria laughed,"Breakfast's getting cold"She announced.

Damian started eating immediately.

Luca stared his beautiful pregnant wife whose mood swings were frustrating hell out of him.

He saw her eyebrows arched together.

"Are you okay?"He asked, concerned.

"I'm just tired"

"I warned you not to fall pregnant again but you wouldn't listen,now, the baby's stressing you out"

"She isn't"Aryann snapped.

"Daddy said you should never be stressed out,the baby's doing that to you, is she bad?"

"No"Aryann retorted, calmly."Daddy's just being paranoid"

Luca gasped,"Paranoid?"

"Can't we ever eat breakfast in peace?"Maria snapped and they went quiet again.

She knew the couple still had to talk things out before returning to their right senses.

"I'm full, Grandma,may I be excused?"Damian asked, politely.

"Of course, sweetheart"Maria replied and Damian scurried off.

"I'm full too"Aryann announced.

"At least for five minutes then you'll start asking for steaks or waffles or......"He paused realizing that he shouldn't be teasing her right now.

"I knew it,you really think I'm fat"

Maria sighed."Can you two please settle this upstairs, I wanna watch Damian's favorite cartoon with him so this is not a convenient place to argue"She warned.

Luca sighed, stood up and strode towards Aryann,he carried her and walked off.

"My point here is that you ain't taking in again and don't try to fool me into believing you're under birth controls after this again"Luca warned,they were both sitting on the bed,seething.

"Well if you can remember,you didn't want children when we got married and when I fooled you into thinking I was under birth controls,you were furious,you didn't want the child but after many nights,you finally dropped the issue and when Damian was born,all your attention flew to him"

"Are we still on that again, I admit,my views about children was wrong but I sincerely think Damian was more than enough bundle of joy for us"

"We got married before Harry,he's expecting his fourth child"She pointed out.

Luca grimaced slightly,"Not everyman wants to be the father of all nation and you think I can ever forget that day when you were in labor,you were literally screaming my name"

"I thought you love it when I scream your name"

"I hate it when you scream my name in pains, I almost died that day"

Aryann giggled,he had cried alot and after everything, when she asked him why he cried that much,he denied ever crying,he denied it to the core.And she could never get him to admit to it.

"I'm hungry"She announced.

"Again?You just ate breakfast"He reminded, surprised.

"I know that look you're giving me,you just said in your mind 'you fat woman"She said mimicking his voice.

"You're not on

my mind"He blurted out.

Her mouth fell open."I'm not on your mind?"

"No…. I didn't mean it that way…. what I'm trying to say is….. that wasn't what I thought about"He said frustratedly.

"Then why did you throw it at my face in my dream?"

"I wasn't in your dream!"He slammed back and stood up.Aryann was driving him nuts,she was overreacting about everything and he was running late for work.

He walked into the dressing room.

Seconds later,he walked out knotting his tie.

"You're going to work?"She asked in disbelief.

"Yes"

"I don't want you to go"

"I'm going'He pressed on.

"It's me, your queen begging you to stay"She reminded.

Luca grinned"I know"

"I'm the love of your life"

"I know"

"I'm your heartbeat"

"Ah! Everyone knows that"He replied staring at the mirror.

Aryann suppressed her lips in a tight line,she wanted to be in his arms throughout today and she knew that the only way to achieve her goal was to use his weakness against him.

"I'm gonna cry"She announced.

Luca turned to face her,"You certainly can't use that against me"

"Well,you can go to work but be prepared to come home and meet my eyes so swollen"She threatened.

His heart clenched just thinking about it.

"You would have been a very good actress!"He exclaimed tugging off his tie.

Aryann smiled."Really? And you would be okay with that?"

Luca thought about the attention most actresses got.

"I take that back"With that he got into the bed.

"So will you finally tell me what this fat issue is all about?It has to do with a book you read or a movie you watched, right?"He asked pulling her up to sit between his legs.As soon as her backside touch his crotch through his pants, tingles of electricity shot through him.

"It was a movie,she was getting fat and her husband started to get less attracted to her"She said sadly.

"You really need to stop watching those miserable movies"He exclaimed.

"I can't help the way I eat,Luca.Does it bother you?"

He tilted her head to look at her face.

"It doesn't at all, you're eating for two,that doesn't mean I would want another child after this but fat or not,you still stir up something in my chest each time I look at you,you definitely ain't fat and your baby bump is beautiful"He said and she felt the sincerity in his words,her lips curled into a broad smile,she rested her head on his collar bone.

He pulled up her shirt and rubbed his hand over her belly.

Aryann felt her baby kicked.

"She's loves to respond to her Daddy"

Luca smiled."And she'll be a beautiful girl just like her mom"

"How beautiful am I now,Luca?"

"It's indescribable,you keep on glowing each day"He slowly cocked his head and stared as her cheeks grew crimson.Up till now,he was glad that he could still make her blush very hard.

"So what will I be doing today at home?"Luca asked.

"Well, the doctor said I need alot of exercises, pulling your hair is one"She said turning around to face him and bitting her bottom lip.

Luca rested his forehead on hers.

"And me thrusting in and out of you is another one"

And then, their lips locked,they nibbled each other's lips once…then twice and for a long time as if they had never kissed before.

A sound came from the door and Aryann quickly sat beside Luca.

Damian walked in.

"Dad,you promised to take me to the park today"He announced.

Aryann sighed but she'd do anything for her sweet little boy.

"Alright,go get dressed,I'll be done in five"He replied.

"Yes!"Damian exclaimed excitedly and ran out of the room.

"Well,baby, I'll try to be home as soon as possible"He promised standing up from bed.

"And I'll await your pleasure"She replied smiling.

She hurriedly held his hand and he thought she was going to tell him something very important.

"Waffles aren't much in the house again and I'm craving for popsicles and meatloaf and watermelon and apples and……"

Luca smiled quite amused.He kissed her passionately.

Then he pulled back.

"My love, I'll buy you everything edible"

The end!